CLONE

CLONE

THE LIFE AND LEGACY OF
AL PARKER
GAY SUPERSTAR

BY
ROGER EDMONSON

alyson books
los angeles | new york

MANUFACTURED IN THE UNITED STATES OF AMERICA.

THIS TRADE PAPERBACK ORIGINAL IS PUBLISHED BY ALYSON PUBLICATIONS,
P.O. BOX 4371, LOS ANGELES, CA 90078-4371.
DISTRIBUTION IN THE UNITED KINGDOM BY
TURNAROUND PUBLISHER SERVICES LTD.,
UNIT 3, OLYMPIA TRADING ESTATE, COBURG ROAD, WOOD GREEN,
LONDON N22 6TZ ENGLAND.

FIRST EDITION: OCTOBER 2000

01 02 03 04 05 a 10 9 8 7 6 5 4 3 2

ISBN: 1-55583-529-5

LIBRARY OF CONGRESS CATALOGING-IN-PUBLICATION DATA
EDMONSON, ROGER.
    CLONE : THE LIFE AND LEGACY OF AL PARKER, GAY SUPERSTAR /
BY ROGER EDMONSON.
    VIDEOGRAPHY:
    1. PARKER, AL, 1952–1992. 2. MOTION PICTURE ACTORS AND
ACTRESSES—UNITED STATES—BIOGRAPHY. 3. GAY ACTORS—UNITED
STATES—BIOGRAPHY. 4. EROTIC FILMS. I. TITLE.
PN2287.P24 A3 2000
791.43'028'092—DC21
[B]   00-045362

COVER PHOTOGRAPHY COURTESY OF JERRY DOUGLAS.

FOR KRJ
SEVENTEEN AND COUNTING

CONTENTS

ACKNOWLEDGMENTS

Special thanks to Jerry Douglas and Robert Richards for their penetrating, in-depth interviews of Drew at various stages throughout his career. I would also like to thank Keith Reiter for allowing me access to hours of Drew's private videotapes. These provided a valuable record of Drew and Richard's domestic life in Hermosa Beach and their travels around the country. I am also indebted to all of Drew's friends and colleagues whom I interviewed for this project, especially Reiter, Janie Schramm, Justin Cade, Joe Cade, Blue Blake, and Ted Sawicki.

This biography was shaped in large part by "Stranger Than Fiction: Like Beethoven Going Deaf," the unpublished autobiographical notes that Drew left in the care of Robert Richards. Thank you, Drew—and Robert.

PROLOGUE

By the mid '70s the heavily politicized gay movement that had grown up in the aftermath of the Stonewall riots was beginning to bog down in partisan bickering. At the same time, gay men—the majority of whom were either disaffected by radical politics or totally apolitical—were beginning to cast about for a new self-image, one that gibed better with their new status as citizens in the "liberated" gay world. For decades gays had been stigmatized as failed men by the heterosexual mainstream. Society, the law, and the mental health profession had generally consigned gays to three basic categories—sissies, hopeless neurotics, and moral degenerates—dismissing them as pathetic perverts running a couple of quarts low on testosterone.

These negative portrayals had tainted the gay world's conception of itself. Even in the privacy and isolation of underground gay culture, the predominant stereotype was the queen—campy master of feminine pronouns, submissive sexuality, and brittle, self-deprecating humor. Masculine-acting men usually self-identified as "trade"—available for sex but not viewed by themselves or by the queens as gay. These men almost invariably adopted the dominant sexual role and rarely, if ever, reciprocated. Clearly, after the revolution a new paradigm was needed. The old stereotypical roles were too negative and ignored the fact that homosexual males were, after all, men.

Some men wanted the new gay to be a politically aware hippie, a man who eschewed the trappings of conventional manliness and reveled in the integration of the masculine and feminine sides of his nature. For others, any behavior that could be construed as womanly was viewed as a symptom of internalized homophobia. This group viewed the post-closet queer as a butch rebel, a man who was in every way the equal of his hetero counterparts—a man as tough and masculine as the old-style queers had been soft and feminine.

This butch perspective quickly gained currency and dominated the scene from the mid '70s through the late '80s. The idea that gay men had the capacity to be just as masculine as their heterosexual counterparts was for many gays a revelation. It was also the easiest path for most gay men to follow. Regardless of their eventual sexual orientation, the simple fact was that men in our culture had, and to an extent still have, only the heterosexual male gender role as a sexual script . There was no available role model for homosexuals.

What gay men did have, however, was a deeply ingrained sense of the non-masculine male's fate. Boys who could conform to society's expectations of the traditionally masculine role were considered manly—successful males. Those who could not were stigmatized as "sissies" or "faggots" and treated with contempt by their peers. Successful adaptation to masculine norms was a means of achieving status in the eyes of other males. The benchmarks of this traditional role are, according to psychologist Joseph Pleck, "physical prowess, same-sex bonding, and a recreational erotic style." Thus, the butch appearance, emotional withdrawal from sexual partners, and a view of sex as a contact sport.

It was in their sexual conduct that gay men most convincingly demonstrated that they had finally become "real men." Gay men selected tricks and performed sexual acts in a hypermasculine fashion. Objectified body parts took on far more importance than incidental attributes such as eye color or warm smiles, never mind emotional connection or social backgrounds. Hot men were hung, built, butch, and ruggedly handsome, sporting short hair and a mustache or trimmed beard.

Thousands upon thousands of gay men flocked to large cities in the post-Stonewall years, celebrating their newfound freedom by flaunting their newfound masculinity. Formerly, the closeted homosexual culture had imitated the pretensions of an aristocratic upper class in their dress and physical surroundings. The new, openly gay male adopted the manly attire and demeanor of the blue-collar worker as a means of expressing his new, hypermasculine sense of self. Of course, gays brought their own unique sensibilities to the process. There was little tolerance for casual sloppiness—hair was cut short, well-groomed mustaches and closely cropped beards were cultivated, gym memberships were purchased, and outfits were carefully tailored and matched. Before long the gays had out-butched the straights, and The Clone was born.

"Clones symbolize modern homosexuality," wrote Martin P. Levine in his groundbreaking study, *Gay Macho: The Life and Death of the Homosexual Clone*. "When the dust of gay liberation had settled, the doors to the closet were opened, and out popped the clone.... Aping blue-collar workers, they butched it up and acted like macho men. Accepting me-generation values, they searched for self-fulfillment in anonymous sex, recreational drugs, and hard partying. Much to the activists' chagrin, liberation turned the 'Boys in the Band' into doped-up, sexed-out Marlboro men."

If this aggressively butch gay male was missing anything, it was a poster boy: someone who could become the model against which successful adaptation to the look—and to the sexual-performance style—was measured. Almost since the beginning of time there had been two distinct schools of thought regarding the male as erotic object—the willowy, pensive youth; and the rugged, muscle-bound athlete. Thanks in large part to Bob Mizer and his Athletic Model Guild, the muscle-bound look had become the modern-day dominant image. In 1967 Rex Colt joined the erotic fray, casting his lot with the Mizer school of thought. From then to the present day, Colt has trained his camera's lens on heroically sculpted male flesh, presenting the viewer with a stimulating, almost unattainable ideal.

One viewer who was most definitely stimulated was a horny tenth-grader in Natick, Mass. This young man, Andrew Robert Okun—"Drew" to his friends—was walking home from the bus stop after school one afternoon when he happened upon a tattered copy of a magazine hidden beneath the bushes in a big field next to the railroad tracks. The area was the local Lover's Lane, a spot for amorous teenagers' trysts and less orthodox sexual encounters. In the magazine was an ad for the Colt Studio, complete with a picture of what young Drew later recalled as a perfect specimen of a man. "His body looked as if it had been chiseled out of marble. Every body part was as perfect as a part could be." Drew took the magazine home with him and "jerked off to it a hundred times." The ad offered sample photos of additional perfect men for a mere $2. The youth took the bait, clipped the coupon, and sat back to wait.

The package, marked PERSONAL AND CONFIDENTIAL, arrived on a Saturday morning. "What I saw in that envelope changed my life. It opened up a whole new world for me. I saw men who were not ashamed to show off their perfect bodies and share them with each other. This was a real revelation for me. I now knew why I had always felt different. These pictures really turned me on."

A few years later, in a seedy West Hollywood bungalow, our young man found himself on the other side of this equation. After an incredibly bizarre and abortive foray into the world of male hustling, Drew was introduced to the legendary Rip Colt. Colt checked the young man out, set up an appointment for some test shots, and handed him his card. The subsequent photo session was a rousing success, and a few months later the gay world was introduced to "Al Parker."

Al was far from what had come to be known as the "Colt standard"—so much so that his debut came with a disclaimer: "This isn't what we usually give you, but you might like it—it might grow on you." Well, it did grow on people, enough so that Al became, in his own words, "the biggest moneymaker Colt ever had."

If asked, fans would most probably mention Al's monstrous member as his most salient feature, the underlying reason for his popularity. True, the Parker prick is the stuff of which legends are made, but his appeal, at least subliminally, went beyond that impressive organ. Al was a gay everyman, someone guys could identify with, not just stand back and gape at in awed silence. With his cropped hair, neat beard, and taut but far-from-overdeveloped frame, he looked like them. The look he embodied was one that could be copied by a majority of the men who were making the new gay social and sexual scene. He was hot, he was handsome, he had beautiful eyes and a mischievous smile. He exuded an obtainable sexiness that depended more on attitude than on yard-wide shoulders, cannonball arms, and swollen pecs. He was perfect fantasy material—the boy next door who just happened to be hung like a horse.

Parker was not only sexy, he was smart. He parlayed his 15 minutes of fame into a career spanning a decade and a half, working behind the camera as often as in front of it, creating a raunchy sexual fantasy world for all those hot clones to aspire to. Later, when the fantasy had gone horribly awry, he became an advocate for safe sex, striving to keep the steam from running out on gay sensuality. Up until his death in 1992 Parker was constantly devising new ways for gay men to assert their sexuality in spite of the AIDS crisis.

So, how did a young, upper-middle-class man from suburban Massachusetts end up as a legend of gay porn, both in front of and behind the camera? It was, as Drew himself suggested wryly, "Stranger than fiction: like Beethoven going deaf."

CHAPTER ONE

Corpses, Knives, and Kinky Sex

Drew Okun was born on June 25, 1952, in Natick, Mass., a town of 20,000 situated on the banks of the Charles River, 18 miles southwest of Boston. His family was solidly middle-class and upwardly mobile. Both parents grew up in Brooklyn, where they were best friends with another couple whose daughter, Janie Schramm, went on to become Drew's lifelong pal. "Both sets of parents were pretty hip," she told me. "Then Drew's folks married, moved to Natick, and became very middle-class." Seymour, Drew's father, worked as a salesman for a chemical company. Drew's mother, Shirley, began assembly-line work welding transistors to boards at a firm that manufactured computer components and within six years would become its vice president.

Drew and Janie were very close as children. "I met him when I was just a baby. Whenever I knew they were coming, I remember I'd get so excited. His folks would come to visit my folks in Queens, and we'd make the pilgrimage out to Natick. Drew did some research once and discovered we were really distant blood relations. We decided to call each other cousins to make it easier to explain our relationship.

"Drew had a rather difficult childhood. He was always a little reserved because his folks were so strict, especially his mom. I remember Drew as being really well-behaved. I was into everything, and his mom would sometimes get mad at me when we were together." Naturally enough, Drew and Janie egged each other on, stirring up all kinds of mischief. "Once we finger-painted the side of my house and got into a whole lot of trouble. Another time we bought some of those explosive caps that go into cigarettes and booby-trapped our parents' packs. They always sat around the table after dinner, arguing about politics and smoking. Drew and I watched and waited while our parents talked. Finally my mom picked up her pack of cigarettes and took one out. She lit up, and BOOM, it went off. We bolted out the back door and ran like hell."

When they weren't getting into trouble they were out playing. "Natick was an old town. There was Revolutionary War stuff all over the place—you know, statues and plaques. Drew was fascinated by graveyards, the older the better. I remember there was also open country around their house, so we were able to run and play in the fields. When Drew came to visit me in the city, we'd play something we called 'Dizzyland.' We'd draw circles and spirals on the street and walk around and around until we were dizzy. He also had a little reel-to-reel tape recorder that we'd use to create Ed Sullivan–type variety shows. We'd imitate singers and comics. He was a great mimic."

The one thing Janie would never have figured Drew to become when he grew up was a porn legend. "He was so, well, mousy as a youngster. He was really into radio. He had a shortwave set and listened to broadcasts from around the world. I remember him as being into all the typical boy stuff, like making scale models. As he got older he was really into cars. His dad was into it also, so it was something they shared. The Okuns bought a new car every year, which struck me as really amazing. Drew loved cars all his life."

Seymour Okun said, "Of all the hobbies Drew had, automobiles were the best. He could identify any car when he was young. He had a '64 Mercury convertible in high school. One time something went wrong with the car, and Drew and his pals took it out into the backyard and rebuilt the engine.

"He was an exuberant kid with plenty of friends, male and female. He went to YMCA camp in the summers. Drew was a good amateur athlete. He played baseball, he swam, he went boating. He did all the things kids his age did. He was always very industrious. He had little jobs when he was in school. I remember he delivered for a pharmacy. When he was growing up there was never any indication he was gay. If he knew, there was no way he let on to us."

He had one older sister, Meg, five years his senior. Janie remembers Meg as "achievement-oriented. She was an excellent pianist, then she became a doctor. Meg was brilliant." Drew was not her equal academically, and he was always in her shadow. Drew admired his sister, although they were never close. In later years they were totally estranged.

In this driven family Drew was something of an odd man out. Nothing in his early years at school marked him for fame and fortune. "If I went back to a high school reunion, I'd be one of those people nobody would remember," he once quipped to a friend. He wasn't the tallest guy in his class or the handsomest or the strongest. In fact, at 5 foot 8—about an inch less, according to some sources—and 140 pounds, he was on the scrawny side and tended toward a nerdy invisibility in the halls and classrooms of Natick High School.

In spite of this, those in the know recognized early on that there was something special about young Drew. There was one place where he was not only visible, he was a standout. This was first brought to his attention when a seventh-grade classmate took a look at him in the showers after gym class, then proceeded to expound on the size of Drew's penis to all and sundry. "I had never really thought about the size of my cock," Drew recalled, "until I was saddled with the nickname 'Pony Boy.' "

Although Drew might not have spent much time dwelling on the size of his private parts, he was, like most adolescent males, quite aware of their function. Masturbation was very much on his mind, and it was an art he spent many long and happy hours struggling to perfect. Being a creative young man, and given the fact that he had a whole lot of organ to manipulate, it was only a matter of time before he stumbled upon the concept of autofellatio.

As he stated years later in an interview with Jerry Douglas, director of award-winning gay-erotic films and longtime editor of *FirstHand* magazine, "Autofellatio is my passion." Later in the same interview, he admitted that the first time he tried it, he got caught. It was one of those rainy Saturdays when there wasn't anything else to do, and plain old masturbation seemed about as exciting as cold oatmeal. He felt something new and different was needed to spice up his adolescent sex life.

"There I was, on the bed with my heels over my head and my schoolbooks piled on my butt to weight it down, sucking my own cock, when my mother walked in with my socks and underwear all folded up real nice and pretty." Mom was unflappable. "Well," she deadpanned, "I'm glad to see those schoolbooks are good for something." For Drew, embarrassment aside, the stunt was less than a raging success. "I can remember when I was doing it that it was like, 'Well, I'm doing it.' But it was not as erotic as it is when you watch somebody else do it."

It wasn't long after this that Drew found the fateful ad for Colt Studios in the field beside the railroad tracks. It was a seminal moment for him, because he was beginning to realize that he was sexually attracted to men. It was something he had been aware of subconsciously for some time, but ordering photos gave undeniable form to his fantasy life.

It also brought into focus one of the great terrors young men in suburbs across America had been dealing with for decades—what if his parents found out? He sent in his money, then he would run home every day after school to see if the package had arrived. "Weeks passed, and my level of anxiety rose. I was deathly afraid it would come and my parents would open it by mistake—and I would be discovered as being gay!" The hapless youngster hadn't considered that possibility until after he had dropped his money into the corner mailbox.

As luck would have it, the package arrived on a Saturday morning. "I was in my room when my father came in holding an envelope marked PERSONAL AND CONFIDENTIAL. I guess every parent knows what kind of stuff comes in envelopes like that. He just stood there waiting for me to open it. My heart was pounding. There seemed to be a silence that lasted forever. Finally, when I had come to the conclusion that there was no way I was going to get around opening the envelope, he just turned around and left. All of a sudden I found religion. To this day, I don't know why he left. I guess he just really didn't want to know." Drew stuffed the envelope into his closet, where it stayed until the following Monday afternoon.

Once he had ascertained that he was alone in the house, he retrieved the envelope and experienced revelation. There were two models in particular who really turned Drew on. "One of them went by the name of Toby. I remember seeing a picture of his dick next to a Coke can—the can looked small by comparison. I developed a crush on him. He was the first man I can remember having true sexual feelings for." The other model was named Erron, a man with an all-American look. "He reminded me of someone, who had probably been the captain of the football team, now gone awry. He looked like the older brother you always wished you had—the one who made you suck him off, then threatened to kill you if you told your parents." Fantasies of these Colt hunks filled young Drew's nights and days.

Drew's sex life remained in the realm of fantasy until the autumn of 1967. In the best Al Parker style, the encounter was far more bizarre and terrifying than anything the 15-year-old could ever have imagined. The scenario had all the trappings of a grade-B horror movie—flyblown corpses, mysterious men with strange accents, dark and abandoned fields, and knives with glittering blades.

It was Friday, October 13, 1967, a crisp autumn day. The trees had just reached the peak of their fall colors, and the grass was rimed with frost. Sister Meg, who was then in her first year of medical school at Boston University, had invited him to join her in the anatomy lab to watch her dissect a cadaver. Drew was contemplating a career in medicine and was intrigued by the prospect of seeing—perhaps even touching—a dead body. He wondered what a dead man's penis looked like. ("Did it get big and hard when they injected the dye into the veins and arteries!")

He caught the bus near the Natick mall and rode into the city. The bus let him off at the Trailways bus station. "It was in a wonderfully seedy part of the city, next to the Playboy Club. My friend Joey had told me that just the week before he had seen a guy in the bus station bathroom jerking off in a stall, using both hands. Even though I was not aware at that time that I was a homosexual, the thought of a man who had a cock big enough to hold and masturbate with both hands was a true fantasy for me." Given the dimensions of young Drew's own cock, this seems a bit odd, but guys are certainly entitled to whatever fantasies they wish to entertain.

He screwed up his courage and dashed into the bathroom. "I pushed the stall door open, my heart pounding with sexual anticipation, sort of like a cross between a headache and a stomachache. All I found was a large puddle of vomit splattered over the bowl and the surrounding floor tiles. I remember there were peas and chunks of carrot. So much for fantasies." He slunk out of the bus terminal and made his way to the university along Washington Street, which ran through the heart of the "Combat Zone." The street was lined with adult bookstores, prostitutes, and dark, dirty little bars. While he walked along, an anxious, sexual feeling churned Drew's stomach—"I wanted to stay and look for Mr. Two Hands"—but he had another appointment that day.

The anatomy lab at Boston University wasn't at all what Drew had expected. "I was under the impression that medical students got all the golden trappings that went along with their future positions." Instead, his sister met him at the entrance to a very old, ramshackle building that smelled of "rotten salami mixed with formaldehyde."

Drew wasn't at all prepared for what he had stepped into. His sister ushered him into a huge room containing row upon row of bodies covered with opaque shower curtains. They were all on gurneys that had troughs running along the sides with holes in them. Under the holes were plastic buckets, placed there to collect the formaldehyde that drained off the bodies.

His sister's cadaver, "Harry," was near the center of the huge room. Like most of the others, Harry had been an inmate of a nearby mental institution, and his body was unclaimed when he died. Drew was fascinated and repulsed at the same time. "I was amazed that the bodies had no refrigeration—no neat drawers to be kept in like you see in the movies." Drew soon identified the strange buzzing sound in the room: Flies' wings beating against the plastic shower curtains. Harry was already infested with maggots. "I remember wondering how many of the people I had passed in the Combat Zone on my way to the university would be on the tables when I began *my* career in medicine."

In spite of the gritty reality, Drew made it through the day. He did not, however, manage a peek at Harry's equipment: "Somehow, I just couldn't violate his dignity by looking down there." All of his lofty ideas about the profession of medicine were fading fast; it was all just a little more intense than he had expected. "By the time I was ready to leave I smelled like a cross between a rotten salami, a condom, and a pepperoni pizza. I still can't eat a pizza or taste a condom without remembering that day."

The sun was setting as he made his way back to the Trailways station, and the chill of impending winter made him shiver. He purchased a ticket and sat down to wait for the bus, wanting nothing more than to get home and wash the smell of death from his body. He did make one last foray into the station toilet. "I checked for old Two Hands, but even the prospect of seeing a monster cock couldn't arouse much enthusiasm in me." Although Two Hands wasn't there, someone else was—lurking in the shadows, watching.

Drew's bus came, and he got on, choosing a seat midway along the aisle, next to a window. There were only about ten other people on the bus, so when a man took the seat next to him, Drew was a bit surprised. He remembered the man as about his own height, with thinning hair, not really attractive, and a bit odd. Nevertheless, Drew didn't move to another seat. He settled back and let the day's events whirl around in his head.

After a few blocks he noticed that the stranger's hand had moved from his lap to his side. "I felt the warmth of his hand as it rested against the outside of my thigh. I glanced over as nonchalantly as I could and saw that he was falling asleep—or so I thought." The man's head had tilted to one side, and his eyes were closed. "At the intersection of Route 128 and Route 9, things turned very strange," Drew recalled. "At the exact place where Route 9 takes a small jog to the left, the stranger's hand jogged left as well, sliding directly onto my crotch. I jerked around to look at him. His head was still tilted as though he was asleep, but his hand was definitely awake. I saw the matronly woman sitting directly across the aisle and wondered if she was aware of what was going on. Apparently she wasn't.

"I didn't know what to do. My heart was pounding so hard, I was sure the entire bus could hear it. Should I say something? Do I scream? Hell, no! This was my first sexual encounter, and a male-on-male one at that. I remember thinking, *Maybe he's got a big one!*"

The man slid his hand along the length of Drew's hard cock, which was full-grown even at the tender age of 15. Drew sensed the electricity as the man examined the prize. "I could tell the guy realized he had hit the jackpot," he recalled, somewhat immodestly. The man obviously knew what he was doing, and Drew decided to let him carry on as he pleased, even if everyone else on the bus figured out exactly what they were doing. "I didn't lose my hard-on for the rest of the ride. The man continued to stroke, squeeze, fondle, and otherwise delight me for the next ten miles. In a way, I was sorry that my stop was coming up." Soon enough, he'd be even sorrier.

"Excuse me, but this is my stop," Drew announced, all blue-eyed innocence, his cock stretching toward his knee. The stranger moved his legs so the youth could get by. The bus pulled up in front of the Natick mall, shut tight by this hour. As the bus pulled to the curb Drew didn't realize that someone was hurrying down the aisle behind him. It never occurred to him that the man who had been fondling him would follow him.

The night was very dark. As Drew crossed the highway to the mall his brain registered the sound of steps on the pavement other than his own, then the cold steel of a knife pressed against his throat. "We are going to take a little detour," the stranger announced in a heavy German accent. Drew barely nodded his head, and the man pulled the blade away from his skin. Drew looked down and saw a medium-size switchblade in the stranger's palm, the blade glittering in the light from a distant streetlamp. He pressed the knife between the youth's shoulder blades and walked him into the field behind the mall.

"I couldn't believe this was happening. The tall grass was heavy with the evening dew. I thought how in this tall grass he could knife me, and it would be months before anyone would find my body. I was just 100 feet from the building where my mother had her computer company. It seemed strange—such a familiar place, now so dark and ominous."

Once in the middle of the field, the stranger told Drew to lie down in the cold, wet grass. Then he told him to take down his pants. "I wondered what he would do if I told him no, but my better judgment told me to do as he said. Still holding the knife, he started to go down on me. I had never had someone suck my cock before, and the sensation of the warm mouth on it made it hard instantly."

Drew liked the feeling but not the circumstances. "I would've loved to knock him out. As he was going down on me I looked up behind me and saw a rock. I seriously considered picking it up and hitting him over the head. I didn't, because I was afraid he'd either bite off my dick or stab me to death. I remember I wanted to take all his clothes and leave him to wander around Natick in the nude."

The stranger unzipped his fly and started masturbating. In that moment Drew's adolescent psychology dredged up a reason for the stranger's behavior. "He opened his fly and revealed the smallest penis in the world. I had never seen another man's penis in my life at that point except in gym class, but I knew. It looked like a wren peeping out of a nest—and that's when it was hard! All of a sudden my anger toward him turned to pity. Here I was, 15 years old with a thick nine inches, and he was a grown man with maybe 2½ inches. He asked me how old I was. When I told him, he seemed surprised that a kid my age could have a cock as big as mine."

Drew tried to regain some control of the situation, thinking that if he acted as strange as the man who was assaulting him, the man might leave. He propped himself up on his elbows and told the man that he'd been cutting up dead bodies all day. "Do I smell funny?" he asked the man. "Cut" and "dead" were obviously the wrong words to use. "I saw a glint in his eye, then I felt his teeth clamp down around my cock. I yelped and told

him I wouldn't let him suck it anymore if he kept biting it—
like I had some control over the situation."

At that point the stranger told him to roll over. The man spit
in his hand and started lubing Drew's ass. The bizarre scenario
coalesced into a moment of sheer terror. "He got on top of me
and tried to screw me, but his cock was so small, and I kept the
muscles of my ass clenched so hard and squirmed around so
much, that he couldn't penetrate my asshole, no matter how
hard he tried."

The man gave up and forced Drew back over onto his back.
"Then, while he jerked off furiously with one hand—holding
the knife in the other—he sucked on my cock until I came. I
had never had an orgasm with another person before. My
whole body shuddered as I blew my load in his mouth. He
devoured it, licking his lips like some kind of uncontrollable
animal. Then he let out a loud scream and came all over my
stomach and underwear."

Drew saw the man's fist clench tighter around the base of the
switchblade he had been holding since the assault began. It was
then that Drew realized his life hung in the balance—the man
would either let him go or kill him. "I thought about my life,
about how young I was and that this could be my last moment
on the earth. I could hear the announcer on the news saying,
'Natick youth slain by sex pervert in open field! Film at 11.' In
a cracked, shaking voice I asked him if he was going to let me
go home now. He looked at me, still twitching with his post-
orgasmic spasms, and said, 'Thank you. You can go.' "

Drew pulled up his semen-soaked pants and ran away, never
turning back to see what the stranger was doing or where he
went. "I couldn't believe what had happened. I remember
debating whether I should tell someone about it." In the end,
the questions—Who was he? Where did he go? Could you

identify him? Why did you let him do this to you?—were more than Drew was willing to deal with. He figured that the man was long gone, and he wasn't willing to face the embarrassment of a confession and the subsequent investigation.

As he got closer to home the scene was already beginning to recede into the realm of nightmare. "As I approached my house I could hear the TV set playing. It was Jackie Gleason doing his stupid impression of the bartender, with that moron Frankie Fontaine as the retarded bar sweep. Everything seemed so trivial and insipid. I remember feeling very dirty. The man's come had gotten sticky, and it was pulling the hairs on my stomach."

He slipped down the hallway to his bedroom and took his clothes off. "I threw my underwear away in the wastebasket by my desk. It seems silly, in retrospect, that I didn't just wash them, but for some reason I wanted to throw them away. I went into the bathroom and took a long shower. After my shower I went to bed. I jerked off four times that night thinking about it. I never did tell my parents, or anyone else, for that matter."

This bizarre first sexual encounter doesn't seem to have left any permanent emotional scars, although it was certainly the first link forged in the kinky chain of sexuality that Drew later celebrated in his X-rated screen classics. Drew continued to tread an undistinguished path in high school, virtually unknown outside of his small circle of friends—uncelebrated except for his "Pony Boy" status in the locker room.

CHAPTER TWO

Woodstock

The next important milestone in the sexual education of young Drew Okun occurred two years later in a muddy cow pasture. This was not, however, just any cow pasture. This was farmer Max Yasgur's pasture in Bethel, N.Y.—a pasture he had rented to promoter Mike Lang, who wanted to stage a concert featuring a handful of rock bands. The event was scheduled to take place August 15–17, 1969, and was expected to draw a few thousand music enthusiasts. Unexpectedly, over 200,000 souls converged on the field that rainy August weekend, overwhelming every facility. At that point in time the counterculture reached its apogee, and an era found its defining moment.

"They're having some sort of musical thing like Tanglewood next week, and you should go," Drew's mother suggested out of the blue one day in the summer of 1969. Young Drew wasn't impressed. Tanglewood conjured images of "listening to Van Cliburn bang away on a piano while sitting on damp grass, getting drunk on wine." However, his mother persisted, insisting that he take her car and invite his friend Richard along on the pilgrimage to upstate New York to a little town called Bethel.

The car was the deciding factor. "Mother's 1965 Shelby Mustang convertible was her pride and joy. She had *never* offered me the car before. It would be worth sitting on wet grass just to get the chance to drive it all that way." The car, a thing of majestic beauty to Drew, had come to his mother quite by accident. She had ordered a stripped-down yellow hardtop with a small engine, but the dealer called to tell her there had been a mistake; if she wanted the yellow hardtop, she'd have to wait. However, she could take possession of the car the dealership had on the lot immediately. "I'm sure a faggot must have put this one together. It looked like it was going 100 miles an hour when it was parked at a curb. It was a beautiful British racing green with snow-white leather seats and black carpeting. It was truly one of a kind."

And so, in a moment of maternal madness, Drew was sent on his way. He wheedled the cost of event tickets, food, and gas money out of his father—"after I listened to one of those Depression-era sob stories about snow and trudging"—and was all set to go. He even managed to suppress his laughter when his mother offered to lend him a few records so he could "bone up on Brahms or Beethoven."

As he pulled out of the driveway on that fateful day his parents stood by the curb, waving. His mother's last request as he drove away was, "Don't let *anything* happen to my car!" Young Drew wasn't worried about that in the least: "After all, I'd had my driver's license for more than a year."

He felt like quite the adult as he and his pal sped along the highway. "Bob Dylan's 'Lay Lady Lay' was the number 1 song at the time, and even today when I hear it, I think of driving that Mustang to my date with destiny." He had expected the roads to be clogged with traffic, but it was clear sailing—for a while. After about three hours, however, they hit traffic. Then, about 25 miles from Bethel, they started to see cars parked on the side of the road. Richard thought they had arrived, but Drew knew it was still a long way to Bethel, and he wasn't about to leave his mother's precious car unattended.

What happened next could never have been envisioned even in a teenager's worst nightmares. They were slowed to a snail's pace—he recalled later that four miles of progress took hours—leaving his mother's gorgeous driving machine idling along in 95-degree heat. "Crowds cheered as they saw us doggedly creep along with the people on foot. We saw other drivers offering rides to the walking masses by allowing them to ride on the fenders and any other unoccupied spaces on their cars."

People were willing to trade joints for rides. Drew had never smoked a joint before. Back home the accepted vice was drinking. Joints were smoked by hippies. "In Natick they still beat you up if you wore bell-bottom jeans." Naturally, Drew accepted all offers of tokes with alacrity, in spite of Richard's scandalized protests. Soon the car was full of people inside and out. "It wasn't long before you could hear the tires scraping the wheel wells, under the weight of hippies loaded with joints. Legend has it that you aren't supposed to get high the first time you smoke grass. Not true. Pretty soon I was reeling."

Just about then a football-cleated guy with long hair slid off the trunk—scraping, chipping, denting, and marring the pristine paint on his mother's gorgeous car. Drew was dismayed, but, fortunately, another joint got passed to him. He took a deep hit and looked around, grinning goofily. "All of a sudden, I was aware that I had the hottest collection of studs I'd ever seen, draped over the hood of my mother's Mustang. I was in seventh heaven."

While Drew was basking in this realization, disaster struck. "Out of nowhere this 1966 GTO came right at us. 'Jump!' someone screamed. The crowd on my mother's car scattered like roaches in the sunshine. Wham! A direct hit to the driver's side. I jumped out of the car, and a very high driver oozed out of the GTO. 'Sorry, man,' the guy slurred, 'but I don't got no insurance.' " To emphasize just how sorry he was, he turned and threw up all over the hood of his car.

While Drew was contemplating the scope of this tragedy, Richard decided to take over the driving. He slid under the wheel, popped the car into gear—reverse rather than first, as it turned out—and the car lunged backward, crashing into a '58 Buick. "I got out to assess the damage. The trunk was dented in such a way that the back bumper, taillights, and gas cap made a demonic smile. I tied the sprung trunk down as well as I could, put up the top, and locked the battered vehicle. I secretly hoped someone would steal it." He rounded up Richard, who was now pouting about his driving gaffe, and joined the walking masses.

From the very first, Drew sensed an incredibly strong sexual aura surrounding the event. As he and Richard drew closer to the festival they passed several small irrigation ponds where throngs of young people were congregating, trying to cool off. "Lots of them had all their clothes off, and I was aware that most of the guys swimming nude had really big cocks. It was the first time I had ever been in a situation to observe a lot of nude strangers." He soon noticed that he was watching the guys rather than the girls and found himself wondering exactly what that meant. He had been looking at those Colt models for a long time, but hadn't quite allowed himself to believe he was gay. Maybe it was just a phase or something. Whatever the case, he couldn't keep his eyes off the guys.

As they walked, Richard complained that he was hungry. He and Drew pooled their resources and stopped at a food cart. Richard figured they'd better stock up, because the crowds were huge and there was no telling when they'd find another cart. Drew wasn't entirely convinced but agreed, if only to get Richard to shut up. After slogging on a bit further they sat down to eat. By this point Drew was anxious to get away from Richard. He wanted to be alone so he could, perhaps, actualize some of the unsettling sexual fantasies flitting through his drug-addled brain. On the other hand, Richard was managing to attract a fair number of handsome guys with all the food they had just purchased. "All of a sudden, we had a group of really good-looking guys around us begging for food. It was like Richard had the part of Elizabeth Taylor in *Suddenly, Last Summer,* and I was Sebastian."

When the food ran out Drew and Richard embarked on the final leg of their journey to the mecca of Woodstock. After walking for what seemed like endless miles they finally got to the gate—what had once been the gate. So many people had shown up that it had been ripped down, and total anarchy reigned.

"I had never seen so many people in one place at one time," Drew recalled. "Everybody was high. Joints were glowing everywhere. I never let one go by without taking a hit." The scene had already begun to take on surreal overtones. "The field was shaped like a natural amphitheater. A layer of straw had been laid over the cow manure left by the former inhabitants." There were toilets dotted around the top of this slope. By 4 o'clock on Friday afternoon the toilets were overflowing with urine, blue water, and what Drew euphemistically referred to as "brown stuff." "Hippies were sitting in the middle of it all, stoned out of their minds, and apparently not minding [the chaos] a bit."

Sprinkles of rain were beginning to fall as Drew and Richard made their way toward the stage. Almost incredibly, they were able to sit right in the middle about three rows back. Drew was elated. "I couldn't believe how good our seats were. I knew we wouldn't want to move from the spot for the whole three days."

Or so he thought. "About then, somebody handed me a very small piece of paper about the size of a fingernail. 'There isn't anything on this,' I said to the guy next to me. 'What do I do with it?' " The guy told Drew to eat it, and so he did.

At that very moment the sprinkles turned into a downpour, sending the crowd scrambling for whatever cover they could find. The revelers had not prepared for inclement weather, and by the time the rain stopped everyone was cold and wet. "The entire field was a slippery mixture of cow manure, urine, water, and human shit. I was soaked and shivering, experiencing the first waves of whatever it is you have on acid. About the same time that Richie Havens started to sing, the speed from the acid kicked in. I couldn't sit still one more second, so I told Richard that I was going to take a walk. It was the last time I saw him that weekend."

As Drew started to walk around he started turning on to the thousands of handsome, hunky men around him. "The drugs had reduced me to pure id. I was aware that I had a raging hard-on, but I didn't care who saw it. As a matter of fact, I was hoping that everyone could see. All I wanted to do was find a gorgeous guy and jump his bones. Woodstock was a sex fiend's wet dream. Guys and girls were sitting in the field getting it on with each other like nobody else was around. Hippies were hanging around the irrigation pools in the nude, swimming and fucking like mink. I had never seen anything like it, and never have since."

While Drew was contemplating this miraculous scene his eye was caught by a shiny, black 1958 Cadillac hearse. "On the door in gold script was a sign that said HELL'S ANGELS. I went closer to take a look at the interior and was startled to see a figure in the back—in the nude. He was magnificent, about six feet tall with piercing blue eyes. His hair was jet-black, falling halfway down his back. His chest hair swirled around his nipples and looked like it had been brushed so every hair was perfectly in place. His belly was a rippling washboard. Our eyes met—it was as if I was in a trance. With his foot he kicked the door handle, and the heavy door opened a crack. I opened the door, and two Plexiglas crosses lit up on either side of the car, illuminating the naked hunk inside.

"He went right for the buttons on my jeans. I remember thinking that it was the first time I was going to have sex with a man that I wanted to have sex with. I had always wondered whether I would think back to that time when I was 15 and freak out. I didn't. What was happening seemed instinctual, totally natural. Here I was, in the back of a Cadillac hearse, having sex with a Hell's Angel. I was tripping.

"His cock got hard even before he got my pants off. He pulled me on top of him, and we rolled around in the back of the hearse. With me on top he pulled my pants down and thrust my hard cock into his mouth. It went all the way down his throat with ease. His warm mouth on my cock was perhaps the best feeling I had ever had. I started thrusting it in and out as hard as I could to see if there was any limit to the abuse the man could take. It was as if he were the perfect sex machine. Not once was I able to make him gag or miss a beat.

"While I did this his dick was rock-hard, thumping against his rippled stomach. I truly thought I had died and gone to heaven. Then I flipped around so I could suck his dick. I wasn't as good at it as he was because I hadn't had the practice he'd obviously had, but I did my best."

Ratcheting the fantasy up another notch was the fact that "he was uncut. I marveled at the way the skin slid up and down over the shiny purple head, alternately covering and uncovering the slick prize. I realized that this most private part of him was only exposed for a few seconds at a time—and collectively for only a short period during a lifetime. And here I was, sharing some of that wonderful time with this perfect specimen of manhood." And so began Drew's lifelong obsession with foreskin.

"He flipped me onto my back and held my hands firmly over my head while he plugged my face with his veiny cock. Then he slid back between my legs and went down on me again. When he did he let out a big groan and started spurting. He shot a heavy load. It came out in huge bursts, flying over my head and hitting the partition that separated the back of the hearse from the driver's seat. I couldn't wait any longer. I shot my load into his hungry mouth. It felt like it went on forever. It was the best moment of my life up until that point."

Afterward they chatted, and Drew learned that the man followed the Hell's Angels around in the hearse, carrying gear and spare parts. Drew looked around, taking it all in. At that moment he swore that he would have his own hearse someday. The pair spent the rest of the weekend together, fucking in the back of the hearse and listening to music. After Woodstock Drew never saw the man again, although he thought of him often.

Meanwhile, the rain never let up, and Woodstock "turned

into an ordeal to live through. I tried to find Richard, figuring he would have remained anchored to the spot I had left him in, but the whole crowd was as liquid as the manure patch beneath its feet. I hoped he was having experiences of his own." After the concert ended, Drew remembered very little about it beyond the drugs and the atmosphere of sexual abandon. "I remember Joe Cocker and Jimi Hendrix, but I couldn't remember where I left the car." When he finally found it Richard had left a nasty note telling Drew that he had hitchhiked home and wasn't going to help pay for the damage to the car.

When Drew pulled into the driveway of his home his folks were standing in the den window, watching. "There's no way to describe their faces when they saw the Mustang limp into the drive. They had been watching the whole drama unfold on the nightly news with Walter Cronkite. It had been described as a disaster zone, so they were happy to see me in one piece."

They were even reasonable about the damage to the car. The repairs cost over $2,000, a princely sum at the time. They never mentioned the cost but did suggest that Drew get his own car. He bought the "biggest, blackest 1959 Cadillac hearse you ever saw. I was not allowed to park it in the drive. My folks bought an electric garage door opener, which— under penalty of death—I had to activate as soon as I rounded the corner onto Brookdale Road. I even had to back the car in so it looked like a normal Cadillac, in case a neighbor saw the door closing."

Life returned to normal for a while. His senior year began, and instead of just being the weird kid, Drew became the weird kid who drove the hearse. Then about three months after Woodstock, a fellow student came running up to Drew in the halls at school. "You're a goddamned star!" she screamed at him. He asked what she was talking about. "Have you seen the movie poster for *Woodstock*?" He hadn't. "You're in it! You're right in front! You're the most famous person this school has ever had! You're a real movie star!"

By the end of the day everyone knew that Drew Okun was featured on the poster for the movie. "I was the coolest dude in school. It wasn't long before Richard found me in the hall. He was livid. 'You sat there for 15 fucking minutes, and you got into the movie poster! I go to the shitter for five minutes and miss everything! Then you disappear for the rest of the weekend while I suffer for three days in the same place and get nothing!' " Richard never spoke to Drew again. "I loved the notoriety. I think it planted the seeds for greater things to come."

CHAPTER THREE

Breaking Away

Shortly after his Woodstock adventure Drew's life was thrown into chaos. His mother, at age 42, was diagnosed with lung cancer. Unfortunately, her illness was already quite advanced. Aggressive chemotherapy and unsuccessful treatment with trial drugs put a tremendous burden of stress on the family. In spite of their efforts Mrs. Okun was dead within a few months. It made Drew realize just how short life could be. "She worked very hard, made lots of money, and didn't get to spend a cent of it. What the hell was life about, anyway?"

Still reeling from his loss, Drew went to college. He was expected to pursue a career in medicine "not because I wanted it, but because of all that Depression-era crap about kids having what their parents couldn't. In my family, either you became a doctor, or you left the country." He enrolled at Boston University to appease his mother's spirit and began the arduous course of study required to become a physician.

As Drew soon discovered, Boston University was a hotbed of

political activism. "The Vietnam War was raging, and not a day went by without demonstrations and riots taking place." He lived in a big dorm complex, and as a part of the campus disruptions that took place throughout the year, a bomb threat was called in to the dorms every night. By law, the dorms had to be cleared while police searched the rooms. "I had to walk down 13 flights of stairs and stand in subzero weather in my pajamas on the football field while they searched all 975 rooms in the complex. At about 6 A.M. they would let you walk back up all those stairs, and you'd have to get ready to go to class. It was that way every night for the whole year."

The radicals won their victory—there was so much turmoil that the school was closed the following May. The students were given 24 hours to clear out. They were told that perhaps they could come back in September to take their final exams. "It didn't take a college degree to realize this was a supreme rip-off. In the year I was there I didn't learn a thing except how to make a bomb threat."

From the first, Drew's foray into the world of medicine seemed ill-fated. The smelly corpses and decidedly unglamorous surroundings he had encountered on the visit to his sister's anatomy lab didn't bode well for him. In addition, "I had a vomit phobia. If a patient ever came into my office and puked, I would probably jump up on my desk and scream like an elephant seeing a mouse in some cartoon. It all stemmed from a trip to the New York World's Fair in 1964." Drew had been stuck in line on an escalator, waiting to enter an exhibit, when the kid next to him threw up all over him. "It was a Technicolor yawn, if you know what I mean. There was nowhere to run. I was trapped. The kid's chili dog came flying at me with break-neck speed. *Blap!* All over me! It took what seemed like hours to get me off that escalator and into a shower."

The vomit phobia, coupled with what he knew of his sister's educational traumas, provided a good enough excuse for Drew to give up the idea of medicine as a profession. "It had been the most miserable time of my life. I was doing something I hated to make a dead person happy! I kept telling myself that life is too short to deal with this shit."

Drew decided to seek his fortune in another arena. First, however, Drew wanted to let his father know about his new plans even though he was certain to disapprove. "I went home and flatly told my father how I felt. Much to my surprise, he told me that he had hated school himself and that very few people ever end up working in the field in which they earn their degree. Since I didn't want to be a doctor, he figured I'd survive without a piece of paper. He was, however, worried about the draft. He didn't want me to become cannon fodder."

Keeping in mind the fact that he could go to Canada if need be, Drew packed his belongings, scanned the ride board at the school, and found a guy who was going to the West Coast. "Ever since I was a kid I had always wanted to be in California. I arranged to stay with my college roommate. He lived in Beverly Hills, so my first destination was Los Angeles." The roommate's father was an advertising executive for Kellogg's, and Drew was suitably impressed by the family's wealth. "I'd never been exposed to that kind of money. I was just a sheltered kid from rural New England, and their house was literally one of those mansions you saw at the beginning of *The Beverly Hillbillies* on TV."

Drew was beginning to think he wanted a career in the film industry, and Beverly Hills seemed the perfect introduction. The morning after his arrival he took a long walk. "I loved the city and was excited about the prospect of living there. I could go to film school, get a job at a big studio, and overnight be a huge Hollywood sensation! I could live in a big house in Beverly Hills, and life would be wonderful." All in all, a good and simple plan.

Still floating on a fantasy cloud, Drew visited San Francisco to see an old high school friend who was living there. He was instantly hooked. Not only was the weather nicer than back East, the city also offered a burgeoning gay subculture where Drew could further explore the sexual nature he had been battling since puberty. "I knew what I wanted—men—but I kept trying to be straight. It was the sort of thing most gay guys went through back then. You think you're the only person on earth who wants to have same-sex relations, so you can't admit it to anyone. So you want it even more."

By 1971 San Francisco was already becoming a gay mecca, and Drew had no difficulty finding the action he craved. It was easy to meet people on the streets and in the parks even for a shy teenager. "It was scary at first, but it was so sexy. Just looking gave me a hard-on, which gave guys an idea of what I had between my legs. Any doubts they might have had about going with a scrawny kid like me usually dissipated when my cock started reaching down my leg. I'd have sex with these really hot guys, then go back to my friend's place and pretend I'd been out sight-seeing."

After a few weeks of this newfound freedom Drew was certain that California was the place for him. Before he could make a clean break, however, he needed to resolve some complications at home. At this point in his life Drew was still involved with his high school sweetheart. "He told me he was thinking about getting married at one point," Cousin Janie told me. She, however, was skeptical. "I think he was just going through the motions—you know, going along with the program. I mean, when he decided to pursue another path he became a gay porno star. How committed to marriage and the straight life could he have been to begin with?"

Committed or not, Drew's desire to be heterosexual had led him to a serious involvement. Ann was an Italian Catholic girl with very strict, very traditional parents. "She had no idea what I was going through, and I knew she wanted to get married. Her parents liked me, and we all got along great, but I knew it wouldn't be fair to go ahead and get married, then have her find out I was gay, so I kept putting her off."

While Drew was in California strange things were happening in Natick, things that would bring his relationship with Ann to a crisis and send his life spinning in new directions. Perhaps she was maddened by the summer heat, or perhaps she was just getting the message that she and Drew weren't going to spend the rest of their lives together in wedded bliss; whatever the case, in a rebellious moment Ann took up with a wild crowd and got herself in serious trouble.

She went out one afternoon with a couple of her new friends and got involved in an armed robbery. One of these new friends, Johnny Ames (bolder than he was bright) decided to rob the gas station where he had been having his car serviced for years. When he emerged from the office after supposedly paying his bill, he had a gun in his hand and cash was falling out of his pockets. As the larcenous trio fled the scene Johnny threw the gun into an empty lot. Needless to say, the gas station attendant recognized Johnny as a regular customer and was able to tell the police exactly where he lived.

In the meantime, Johnny convinced Ann to return to the vacant lot and retrieve the gun used in the crime so Johnny could melt it down and destroy the evidence. Incredibly, Ann agreed to do it. "God knows what kind of drugs she was on. It must have been a real scene. There they were, trying to melt a gun with a propane torch, when the police broke into the house and arrested all of them for armed robbery."

Ann's father, the good Italian papa, heard the news about his daughter's arrest while at work. In a fury he raced out, jumped into his brand new Monte Carlo, and headed to the jailhouse to bail out his errant child. He never made it. As he started out of the parking lot he had a massive coronary, crashed into a line of parked cars, and died on the spot. "The story goes that they had to break his fingers in order to get them off the steering wheel so they could take him to the funeral home."

And so when Drew returned from his trip to California, everything was in chaos. "I called to tell Ann about my trip. When I reached her home I could hear people crying in the background. I was told the basic outlines of the story and went right over. I had recently lost my mother, so I knew how Ann felt. I felt so sorry for her that that night we went to bed together. It was the first and only time, but good Italian Catholic girls are very fertile. Naturally, she got pregnant."

The conflict was immediate and seemingly irreconcilable. Drew desperately wanted to get back to California and start a new life for himself. Ann now desperately wanted to get married to the father of her child. Drew was at a loss. Whatever the outcome, he needed money, so he took a job at a large store called Boston Baby Carriage.

While assembling baby cribs, of all things, Drew evaluated his options. Years later, talking to interviewer Robert Richards, Drew ruminated about the choice he had made. Had he done the right thing? "I wonder what my sexual choice would have been had I known what the years would bring. Would I have chosen to be gay? Did I have that choice? Unless you're a totally dedicated bottom, in which case you can't do without a man, it almost seems as though there is a choice. I just don't know."

On the one hand, Drew really did love and respect Ann. On the other hand, he knew deep down that his primary sexual attraction was to men. "I knew that to marry her, have a family, and be miserable wouldn't be fair to either of us. She was a great girl and really deserved more than I could offer her. I told her I couldn't get married and I still planned to go to California, but that it was her decision regarding whether or not she wanted to have the baby. She opted for an abortion."

Abortion was still illegal, and it was very difficult to find a person to perform the procedure. After asking around discreetly they heard of an abortionist in New York City. "Our instructions were to fly into JFK International Airport and look for a man who had a button on his lapel that read '300.' After finding him, we were taken to a van and locked inside. For all the world, it was like a bad James Bond movie. We had no idea where we were going, and they wouldn't tell us the destination for fear we were undercover cops or something."

After a two-hour drive they arrived at an industrial park somewhere on Long Island. The building was obscured among electronic assembly plants. "I felt wary. The place didn't look clean and certainly didn't resemble a hospital. We went inside, and I sat in a waiting room full of hostile parents, all of whom stared at me contemptuously. It was obvious that they saw me as a perfect example of the kind of louse who had defiled their daughters. Hell, at least I was there to go through this ordeal with Ann instead of just dumping the problem on her mother. Visions of coat hangers danced in my head the entire time she was in the operating room. I could see some dirty old man unbending a hanger, leaving just the hook at the end so he could snag the little bastard and pull it out by its head. It was not a good time."

After Ann finally emerged from the rear of the building, they had to find their own way back to the airport. "It was obvious that she was in pain, but we never discussed what had gone on. I still find it hard to believe that I would now be the father of a child in its 20s if things had been different. Still, I thought then and still think now that we did the right thing." Three months later Drew loaded up his hearse and, with $1,000 in his pocket, took off for California to pursue his destiny.

CHAPTER FOUR

Playboy Mansion West

The day Drew left home to pursue his future in California, he left behind more than just his family and friends. In many ways, he left himself behind as well. Drew found out that when Tom, the classmate he was planning to travel with, told his friends about the upcoming journey, they asked him what on earth Drew Okun had to offer as a friend. This brought it home to Drew in no uncertain terms that he really was an outsider. "I was not all that popular in high school. I was just the weird kid with the hearse, and until that poster for the movie *Woodstock,* nobody there even knew who I was."

Drew decided the move to California was the perfect opportunity to remake himself. "If I was going to move so far from home, why repeat the same old mistakes? It was my chance to start over and become somebody I wanted to be."

The recent death of his mother had shaken him profoundly. Every time he thought of her he saw a life unfinished. She had been successful but had died before she could spend any of the money she had made. In a somewhat morbid frame of mind, he dredged up a list of short-lived relatives and figured he had no time to waste. "In my family it seemed that if you lived past 40, you were doing really well. Longevity wasn't one of our strong traits. I had a premonition that I wasn't going to make it past the age of 40 myself. I could clearly see my life up to that point, but after that there was nothing but a big blank." (In fact, Drew died two months after his 40th birthday.)

Given that dismal track record, Drew wasn't inclined to waste any time. As he drove west he formulated a new, and somewhat cynical, philosophy to live by. "I was going to have a fabulous life. I was going to milk it dry, taking everything there was to take. You are the driver of your own destiny, and if you don't make your life interesting, then it won't be interesting. Face it, you are the only person who really and truly cares about you. The way I saw it, everybody was responsible for his own orgasm." Thus, Drew made the decision to have fine and frequent orgasms, and in that, he succeeded beyond his wildest dreams.

Drew and his buddy made their way to Los Angeles, land of sunshine, beaches, and orgasms. They had loaded their possessions into the hearse and were towing Tom's Volkswagen, creating an unwieldy caravan over 30 feet in length. Maneuverability was minimal, a quirk that was instrumental in opening the next chapter in Drew's life.

As they drove along the Pacific Coast Highway the two travelers spotted a blond bathing beauty doggedly waving passers-by into the parking lot of a tacky waterbed store in Hermosa Beach. Tom, thoroughgoing heterosexual that he was, wanted a closer look, so Drew pulled off the highway. The blond turned out to be less than a beauty, but she had served her purpose. "The hearse with the Volkswagen trailing along behind was too long to turn around, so we continued down the street. There was a FOR RENT sign on what looked like a nice apartment building. Tom and I saw this as a portent, so we took the apartment."

Drew found work at a Mobil station on the Pacific Coast Highway, which paid the rent but was hardly what he had envisioned as his life's work. Luckily, he wasn't required to pump gas for long. He met the guys who rented apartment number 6 in his building and learned that they worked as butlers for *Playboy* magazine publisher Hugh Hefner. They regaled Drew with glamorous stories of wild parties and even wilder movie stars cavorting at the Playboy mansion.

Hefner was the man of the hour in the early '70s, and his weekly Sunday parties were legendary. In 1971 one of Hefner's lady friends had found an appropriately grand six-acre estate in Beverly Hills, and Hef had set up a West Coast base of operations. The mansion, built in the '20s by a department store magnate for his young wife, was a replica of an English estate.

Drew found his new friends and their job intriguing, so when an opportunity arose to work a party at the mansion, he jumped at it. He was, in his own words, "ready to lick the plates of those rich stars and starlets as they came back to the kitchen."

He went out to buy a pair of black slacks and a white shirt for his debut, discovering that this little gig bestowed celebrity by proxy. "The girl behind the counter asked why I needed the items, and when I told her that I was going to work for Hugh Hefner she got very excited. I liked the attention. Here I was, in California for only a few weeks, and already I had gained access to the Playboy mansion and would soon be rubbing elbows with Hollywood royalty."

Drew drove the old hearse through the mansion's gates and

reported for duty in the kitchen. The staging area at the back
of the house was bustling with activity. Drew was introduced
to the house manager, Pauline, and to the head butler, Tom. "I
was told to fold napkins. There was nothing at all glamorous
about the job, and it was obvious that the people who worked
there were working hard. All I wanted to do was see the stars.
I folded my napkins, wiped glasses, lugged ice, and set out the
silverware. In between tasks I caught glimpses of the guests—
Warren Beatty, James Caan, Cher, Laurence Harvey, and a
galaxy of others. It was a who's who of Hollywood. I thought
to myself that someday I would be a guest myself rather than
an employee."

The young man was overwhelmed by the debauched
grandeur of it all. The property, as Drew described it, was more
a Busby Berkeley vision of Hollywood than real life. "As you
entered the house you came into a great hall that was two stories tall, lined all around with little balconies. The walls were
paneled in mahogany, and the floors were highly polished marble. There was a stairway that curved up from both sides of the
hall to a landing where there was a large polished brass sculp-
ture in the form of a woman's cunt. I was told that if you had
a personal message for Hef, you would write it on a piece of
paper and put it in the lips of the cunt.

"It seemed like a real kingdom to me. There was an aviary
filled with exotic birds from all over the world. Llamas, emus,
and various types of monkeys had the run of the grounds. A
pond was stocked with rare fish that cost as much as $3,000
each. There were 70 full-time employees who catered to Hef's
every whim.

"Hef rarely left the property, because once he went into the
outside world he was just another mortal. At the mansion he
was God. People literally shook in fear when he walked by.

Even his children had to make an appointment to see him, and when the appointed hour came he might just cancel without warning. His friends often had to play the part of court jesters, entertaining Hef. He never changed out of his pajamas, never smoked a pipe more than once, and was never, never without a sweating Pepsi in his hand."

The mansion was a palace of excess where consumption was conspicuous to the point of parody. Even Drew, dazzled by it all, couldn't help feeling slightly repulsed. "There was a never-ending supply of crab, shrimp, and lobster. I couldn't believe what I saw that first night. I mean, guests would take one bite out of a Maine lobster and throw the rest away. Aspiring starlets would cram their pockets and purses with food they would then take back home and live on until the following Sunday, when they would return and do it all over again."

In the midst of the madness Hefner was conspicuously absent. Drew learned that he usually stayed upstairs in his private quarters playing backgammon. If he showed up at all, he would just stroll through the party in his pajamas long enough for everyone to glimpse him, then disappear.

The bizarre atmosphere surrounding the mansion and its elusive owner appealed to Drew. He genuinely enjoyed watching the Hollywood glamour crowd at play and wanted an opportunity to see more. His wish was granted. The next day he got a call from Tom, the head butler, asking whether he would like a permanent position. Drew jumped at the chance.

He quickly discovered that it wasn't his napkin folding skills that had led to this summons; it was one of his other qualities that had been spotted, evaluated, and deemed worthy. Tom was willing to offer Drew the job—as long as Drew was willing to offer something in return. "When I assured him that I could handle the job, he asked me whether he could handle my knob. I looked at him stupidly, thinking I hadn't heard him correctly. Before I knew what was happening I was getting an expert blow job. Tom dropped to his knees and went all the way down to the base of my cock in one smooth move. It was Woodstock revisited. I came in nothing flat. He wiped his mouth on his starched white shirt cuff and told me I'd been hired. I was requested not to reveal the details of the interview. He interviewed me almost every day for the entire time I worked there, and I never failed to satisfy."

Drew soon found out that almost all the butlers on staff were gay, primarily because Hef knew gay men wouldn't be a threat to the dubious virtue of his "bunnies." The women who traveled with Hefner back and forth between Chicago and Los Angeles required constant attention. They were virtual prisoners, on the payroll only so long as they stayed on the property. If they left to shop or enjoy free time, they didn't get paid. As a result "there were lots of bitchy beauties on the grounds, demanding that the world be brought to them right by the pool, day and night." There was more than enough to do to keep a butler busy.

In addition to the bunnies and the butlers there was what Drew referred to as the "goon squad," made up of washouts from FBI training school. It was primarily employed to keep the butlers from talking to the bunnies. Any employee caught talking to a bunny would be fired on the spot. The guys eyed each other, the bunnies resorted to lesbian encounters to relieve tension, and the goons kept a watchful eye on everyone. "It was a frustrated bunch of sex perverts stuck on a six-acre paradise known as Playboy Mansion West."

Frustrating it may have been, but the job was undeniably glamorous to someone who aspired to be a part of the Hollywood scene. It was a real-life version of *Upstairs,*

Downstairs, and the staff quarters buzzed with gossip day and night. Even with stars and celebrities coming and going all the time, the staff occasionally got genuinely excited about some of the guests.

One of these individuals was Elizabeth Taylor. "I don't know what it is about her that excites so many people, but when we heard she was coming to the mansion we all got crazed." The visit occurred during her marriage to congressman John Warner, when her weight had ballooned out of control. She wasn't looking too good, but she was still Liz Taylor, so whenever she passed through a room the staff would stop work and just stand and stare. She was not amused. "After a few hours of that she stopped dead in her tracks and screeched, 'What the hell are you all looking at? Stop looking at me! I can't stand it! You're all looking at how fat I am, aren't you?' A memo went out immediately, to the effect that when she was approaching the staff was to disappear. That meant hiding wherever possible. When her heavy little footsteps were heard we all dove for cover. If she was at all attentive, she would have been able to see shadowy forms huddled behind the couches or feet sticking out from beneath the hems of the drapes. She was Lady Godiva, and we were the peasants. I was very disappointed."

Another woman of distinction was Linda Lovelace, famous for her role in the X-rated classic *Deep Throat.* Whenever she visited, an enormous bloodhound would be brought from its pen to the pool house for fun and games. "One of my jobs was to retrieve the dog. It was a very large dog, and it was very eager to please. The only problem was that it never saw anyone unless it was summoned to perform, so as soon as it saw me it would begin its act. I'd be dragging the beast across the manicured lawns, getting my leg humped along the way. Afterward, I would have to go to the pool house and clean up. It was always a horrible mess, and I never did figure out exactly what they did in there. Through it all Linda was very sweet and very pretty. I never realized she was being coerced to do these things until I read later that she claimed she was forced to make the movies against her will."

John Lennon also made his way to the mansion while Drew worked there. "He had just separated from his wife, Yoko Ono, and was in a bad space. While I watched him one afternoon I saw him put a cigarette out on a Jackson Pollock painting. I don't think it changed the painting all that much, but I was surprised that someone who considered himself an artist would do that."

Drew also dredged up interesting tidbits on other celebrities. The bunnies would often kiss and tell, much to the delight of the staff. However, Drew found out about one guest, Warren Beatty, firsthand rather than through one of the loquacious bunnies. Hef was fascinated by video, which was then a new technology. He, perhaps not surprisingly, was something of a voyeur, and with that in mind had installed video cameras throughout the mansion. One evening Drew tuned in to a camera mounted in a shower and saw Beatty nude. "Yes, it's true. Warren Beatty has a really, really big one, and so does Tom Jones."

One guest brought about the end of Drew's career as a butler and put him, literally, in Hugh Hefner's closet. Comedian Bill Cosby came into the breakfast room one morning after a game of tennis. When Drew went to wait on him he tripped on a tennis ball and dumped a glass of ice water into Cosby's lap. Drew apologized and brought another glass. "I slipped on another ball, and the water went all over him again. We both laughed, me more than him, and I cleaned up the mess." The third time around Drew got tangled in the racket. When he laughed this time, he laughed alone. "So ended my stint as a butler. I didn't mind because I preferred being served rather than serving."

Luckily, there was another employment possibility available at the mansion. Someone was needed to show sixteen-millimeter films to the guests if they requested them and to videotape television programs for Hefner's private viewing. (This was before the advent of VCR technology.) Hefner had a roomful of studio video equipment set up in a closet off his bedroom. Drew was in this closet for up to 18 hours a day and had the dubious pleasure of observing Hefner up close and personal. "Seeing as how I was only five feet away from him all day long, I was the easiest person to contact if something went wrong. The man had a temper, and something was always going wrong. He would scream and yell at me about things I had no control over, and I would have to find the proper person to correct the problem. I spent my time either stressed to the max or bored brainless.

"I worked maybe three minutes in an 18-hour shift. There were many times he would walk into the room and find me doing some very strange things." None of these strange things, which ran the gamut—hundreds of push-ups a day, studying for his classes at UCLA film school, virtuoso bouts of masturbation—were considered serious enough to demand removal from the premises.

Drew, stuck in a boring job with virtually nothing to do, decided that he needed to spend his time learning something constructive. After rejecting foreign languages and mathematics as too dull, he decided to dabble in the occult. His choice was not entirely random: Drew had heard gossip about the original occupants of the mansion and became intrigued. Sara Lutz, bride of the man who built the mansion, had fallen from one of the balconies surrounding the great hall during an argument with her husband and died, her brains dashed out on the cold marble floor. It was rumored that her ghost wandered the hallways and lonely bedrooms when the house was empty. Hefner discounted the tale, but some of his guests weren't so sure. Drew decided it might be interesting to contact Sara and while away the empty hours with her. It turned out to be a perilous undertaking worthy of a James Whale movie.

"I bought a deck of tarot cards and a copy of the cabala"— a system of Jewish mysticism and magic used to interpret Scripture—"and started to study. I told others on the staff what I was doing, and they all wished me luck except for Chuck, the chauffeur. He told me that he had encountered Sara several times and that I shouldn't mess with something I didn't understand."

Chuck's advice was too sensible to take. Drew hunkered down to study the cabala, attempting to learn spells that would help him contact the dead. "I would focus on her spirit and talk to her. One night when everyone else had returned to Chicago and I was all alone in the house, I swore I could hear a banging on one of the bedroom doors in the mansion. It was the room next to the master bedroom—which, I later learned, was Sara's room.

"I was taping an episode of *Leave It to Beaver,* and it was 2:30 in the morning." (Drew's life had recently been complicated when Hef became convinced that Ken Osmond, the actor who played Eddie Haskell on *Beaver,* and porn star John Holmes were one and the same person. Since Hef had something of an obsession regarding Holmes, he demanded that Drew get up in the middle of the night, when reruns of the sitcom were aired, and record them.) "I was listening to the audio on the show, so I wasn't paying much attention to the banging. Then I heard it again. As it became more insistent I opened the door of my room and looked out into the hallway. The sound became deafening. I felt like Julie Harris in *The Haunting!*

"The only people on the grounds, besides me, were the security guards, and they were housed in a separate building at the entrance to the property. I called them and told them to knock it off, figuring that maybe they were doing it to spook me. They denied it and said they'd be up to investigate. When I hung up, the pounding started on my door so fierce that I feared the wood would splinter. I could literally see the thick panels buckling. I was scared shitless. I mustered all my courage and threw the door open, but there was nothing there." When the security guards arrived, guns drawn, all was quiet—so they left, convinced Drew was putting them on.

"Two days later there was a fire in the bedroom Sara had slept in during her lifetime. It was so hot, it literally melted everything in the room. It should have spread and destroyed the entire house, but it didn't. I was convinced that Sara was getting stronger and that I was the cause of it. I went back to my books and studied harder than ever. How could I resist?"

Drew's dabbling in the occult came to a spectacular climax on Halloween night, 1973. He was alone at the mansion, charged with the responsibility of recording *Funny Girl,* which was making its television debut that night. Hef really wanted a copy of the film, so there was to be no reprieve.

"I was in the video room, listening to the movie through headphones—knowing that if I screwed up, my ass would be in a sling for sure. All of a sudden, I was aware of the floor vibrating, like very low notes were being played on an organ. The mansion was equipped with the third-largest privately owned pipe organ in the United States, but there was nobody around to play it. Still, the vibration wouldn't quit. I took off my headphones and checked my equipment, thinking that perhaps the tape heads on the video machines were spinning out of round or something. When I removed the headphones I could clearly hear the organ, off-key and very spooky.

"I grabbed the phone and called for security. They thought I was trying to pull something on them again, but I was screaming at the top of my lungs, so they agreed to come. I was terrified. As I stood in the room, frozen with fear, I could smell faint traces of a woman's perfume, which I had read was a classic ghostly manifestation. I felt like I was on an episode of *The Twilight Zone*. All of a sudden, I was much less intrigued by the concept of meeting up with Sara.

"The guards came, heard the music, and ran downstairs to the room that housed the organ. I followed. As we all rounded the corner and raced into the living room, we could see the organ's keys going up and down by themselves. The three guards and I dashed around the place like Keystone Kops, practically bouncing off each other. Then the music stopped, and it got very cold. You could see your breath, and the air smelled musty, like a damp basement. This cold spot moved around the room, and we ran after it, trying to follow.

"Then we heard a woman's mad laughter. It was as though poor Sara was laughing at the sight of us all scrambling around like clowns. The laughter stopped abruptly, and the temperature returned to normal. It was obvious that whatever it had been, it had left the room. Then the phone rang. It was a guard down at the station, his voice trembling as he told us that he could hear a woman, a crazy woman, laughing at him, but no one was there.

"Later we all sat around the kitchen table, wondering how we were going to explain this in the security log. The guards insisted that it had to be entered, and it was. We all knew it had

happened, even though everyone on staff made fun of us—
except for Chuck, the chauffeur. Hef read the report when he
came back and warned us that if we told anybody about it we
would lose our jobs. This truly had a profound effect on me. I
had never been a religious person, but there was something in
that house. I don't know what it was, but it was there. There
were forces at work there that I didn't understand. Whatever, it
ended my interest in the occult. I have never messed with it
since, even though it did provide the wildest Halloween night
I ever experienced!"

Drew's job as Hef's video technician didn't get any more
interesting as time passed. To make matters worse, the pay
sucked, so Drew was always picking up odd jobs to supplement
his income. Shortly after migrating to California he had ven-
tured off the beaten path with a friend to undertake a venture
Drew later referred to as "Worm World."

As Drew's father recalled, the two were planning to raise worms
as an alternative source of protein. "They had a worm farm in
Venice Beach—this was before he told me he was gay. He could-
n't have been much more than 22. He was still working for
Hefner at the time. He thought this worm farm would be a great
idea, so I invested some venture capital in two sets of worm sup-
plies. He was into making protein food with the worms. They
had bake-offs to find ways of eating the worms. In the end, he
neglected the worms, and that was the end of that." However, as
Drew remembered the episode in a 1979 interview with journal-
ist and illustrator Robert Richards, the worms expired because
when he went to Europe on a holiday, his friend—jealous of his
good fortune—refused to take care of their squiggly friends. In
any case, the worms died, no cookbook-worthy recipes emerged
from the venture, and the project was abandoned.

Drew was still taking film classes and decided to lobby his boss for a job with the movie division of Playboy Enterprises, but was turned down: Hef was used to Drew and had no interest in breaking in another technician. So Drew toiled on in Hugh Hefner's closet, still dreaming of becoming a real part of the hypersexual, money-powered world he was on the fringes of. But Drew's four years at the Playboy mansion ended abruptly. He dared to take the initiative when management couldn't get it together to make a decision—and he paid the price.

The butlers were required to wear heavy wool suits year-round; during the heat of the summer it wasn't uncommon for one of the guys to pass out. Management had solicited designs for a summer-weight suit and even had several prototypes made up so that Hefner could make the final choice. Unfortunately, those in management were so intimidated by Hefner that they couldn't build up the courage to ask him to choose.

"The uniforms hung in a storage closet for almost the entire summer while the butlers were dropping like flies. I finally couldn't stand it anymore and took it upon myself to show the uniforms to Hef. I worked close to him all day, and I wasn't afraid of him. I hung the uniforms all around the video room and left a note asking which one he liked the best."

Unfortunately, when management got wind of his audacious behavior, Drew was immediately terminated. "They told me that they would tell the unemployment office I had been laid off so I could collect unemployment insurance. Since I had been there for four years, I figured that was only fair." However, they lied. When he went to file for unemployment compensation, Drew was informed that he was ineligible to collect benefits because he had been fired. "I was told that I would have to go out, find another job, make at least $300, and then be laid off by the new employer in order to have my benefits paid by Playboy." Drew left the unemployment office breathing righteous fire. "I wasn't about to let those bastards fuck me over and get away with it. Not me. I don't get mad, I get even!"

CHAPTER FIVE

Name That Tune

J ust how the hell could a fellow find a job, earn $300, then contrive to get laid off? While Drew was obsessing over this question and the injustice of his treatment at the hands of Playboy's management, he stumbled across a classified ad that would, he firmly believed, be his salvation. "Earn big money as a game-show contestant!" the ad screamed. "It was the perfect solution. I would go on a game show, earn 300 bucks, and make those bastards pay my benefits."

Drew called the number and was told he would have to pass a test which would determine whether or not he would be a good contestant. He drove into Hollywood determined to succeed. "The game show was called *Name That Tune*. Well, I had seen the show on television often enough to know that most of the tunes they played were from the big-band era, and music had never been one of my strong suits, but I felt confident I could handle it. Besides, I really needed that money. I walked into a room with about 25 other people, and

I was by far the youngest person there.

"We were briefed on the basic rules of the game, then the band started to play some tunes. The band was a small ensemble, more like what you'd expect at a wedding or a bar mitzvah—and they played about as well. After the first six or seven notes the band would stop, and you'd have to identify the title. Have you ever heard the first six notes of Aretha Franklin's 'Respect' on a xylophone? I didn't have a fucking clue."

After missing ten of ten on the tunes, Drew then underwent the personality interview. "I knew they wanted people who were willing to make asses out of themselves. Easy enough, I thought. I'd been doing that for 23 years. I was as bubbly as I could be, jumping up and down and pulling out all the stops to display my acting ability. After they had interviewed everyone an assistant came in with the test results. I had scored lower than anyone else in the room. I had a sinking feeling that this wasn't fated to work out."

Drew sat there watching the people who had scored the highest gloat over their success. The selections were made, and he definitely hadn't been chosen. As he was dejectedly filing out of the room one of the testers asked him what he did for a living. He took a deep breath—and lied. "I work for Hugh Hefner at the Playboy mansion," he replied, his face a portrait of an honest man. "You're on the show Friday night," the tester told him.

Drew was elated. As he drove back to his place in Hermosa Beach he once again began to entertain visions of money and fast cars as he identified tune after tune. That night he was too excited to sleep. "The next day I went to a hypnotist. I had the suggestion planted in my mind that if I had ever heard a song before, I would be able to recall the title. I thought hypnosis was total bullshit, but I was desperate."

On the following Friday Drew drove to the NBC studios in Burbank. Ever the optimist, he brought along three changes of clothes because if you won a game, you came right back for the next show. Drew walked into the studio and met his opponent. "She was a 64-year-old woman named Rose. In her youth she had been a singer with a local band. Rose owned a hotel on Catalina Island, had a Mercedes, and hardly needed the money. Did she realize I was starving? Did she care?"

Drew was blown away by the experience of being in a real TV studio. "It was like being on an acid trip. The grand prize, a Pontiac Tempest, revolved slowly on a turntable in the background. All you had to do to get it was name five tunes in 60 seconds in the bonus round. I was going to win it all!"

Things didn't get off to a very auspicious start. Rose won the coin toss and went first. Her first tune was "Alexander's Ragtime Band." She named it almost as soon as the music started playing. Drew's tune was "For He's a Jolly Good Fellow," and he blanked out. He stood there racking his brain for the answer while his money slowly flowed down the drain. "When the emcee told me the title I felt like an idiot. The hypnosis really was bullshit! Old Rose was leading now ten points to zip."

The second round didn't go much better. The contestants had to spin a wheel, which would indicate the dollar amount their next tune was worth. Drew kept hitting the $25 slot, while Rose kept landing on the top slot, $1,000. Drew got a couple of tunes, but Rose was beating the pants off him, moneywise. His dreams of winning $300 began to seem impossible, never mind driving off with the new Pontiac. By the end of the second round Rose was ahead 20 points to nothing.

For the third round, the person who knew the selection that the band was playing would dash down a runway, pull a bell, and name that tune! Drew figured it would be a piece of cake. "Rose was 64. I was 23. I should be able to run faster and jump higher. After all, I was raised on Wonder bread, the one that built strong bodies 12 ways!" They lined up at the starting line, and the band began to play. Drew didn't recognize the tune. Rose did. "Can you imagine how it looked to see this old lady toddle down the runway? It took her 50 steps to go ten feet! There I was, with my thumb up my rear as I watched the backside of this ancient lady getting smaller in the distance. She got to where the bell rope was, and it literally took her three tries to jump high enough to grab the damned thing. Then she forgot to let go. She dangled in the air, and the audience gasped. When she shouted out the correct answer the audience went crazy. The deck was clearly stacked against me, and they all wanted her to win."

This embarrassing debacle was repeated twice more, and Drew began to despair. "Why couldn't they ask questions like 'How many taillights does a 1961 Chevy Impala have?' I really didn't know a damned thing about music, but this was the only show on TV that gave away cash instead of hair dryers or washing machines. I really needed that magic amount of $300 to get the unemployment insurance and get back at the miserable woman who'd fired me."

Even though Drew was 30 points behind when the last part of the contest began, he still had a chance to turn things around. The last part of the game was called "bid-a-note," and it had made the show famous. The contestants would bluff each other by bidding to name a tune in the least number of notes. The number of notes that were bid would decrease until one contestant was told to name that tune.

Drew was convinced that he didn't have even a ghost of a chance. "Hell, if I couldn't come up with 'For He's a Jolly

Good Fellow,' how could I come up with an answer after being given a clue and three notes?" The round began, and Drew called Rose's bluff at three notes. She listened and drew a blank. "It passed to me. Off the top of my head I said 'Brahms' Lullaby.' I was right, and the audience applauded for me for the first time that night."

The second round was bid down to three notes and again Rose faltered. Drew guessed correctly and began to believe he had a chance to win the competition. "Now I was the under-dog, and the audience was starting to warm to me. Rose was frowning. I was on a high that the best drugs in the world couldn't duplicate. All of a sudden this boring game had come to life like the seventh game of the World Series. The clue was read, and you could have heard a pin drop in the auditorium."

Drew won the round, identifying the song "Jean" from the film *The Prime of Miss Jean Brodie,* which had won an Oscar in 1969. And then Drew heard what he had won: "An all-expense-paid trip for two to New York City, worth over $2,200!" Drew had succeeded. "It didn't matter what happened beyond this point. I had made the money I needed to collect my unemployment." Drew went on to lose the playoff round, and he never got the Pontiac Tempest, but he still had that trip to the big city. "Little did I know, that trip was going to be the turning point of my life."

The next Monday, Drew went down to face the friendly folks at the unemployment office. He was told to fill out some forms and then go stand in line. He was told that there was not a cat-egory for "game-show contestant," so he couldn't collect any money. "I wasn't going to let this lie. The first thing NBC does when you walk through the door is take your Social Security number. Then, if you win, the amount is added to your yearly income. I was going to be paying tax on the value of that trip, so it was income. I went to a lawyer and got a trial date set.

"The day of the trial rolled around, and I dressed in my best suit—which, by the way, had little bunnies embossed in the fabric of the lining. I pled my case in front of the judge, then the government responded. When the judge announced his decision, I realized that I had won. I had also set a precedent— so that if you live in California and are on a game show, you can collect unemployment. For that you can thank me."

CHAPTER SIX

The Beach Bunny and GI Joe

Drew had gotten the better of his former employer (and, incidentally, enjoyed his moment of fame on national TV). But he still had not achieved his primary goal, which was to re-create himself in a way that would leave him content. When all was said and done, Drew Okun was still that nerdy kid from Natick—the weird one who drove the hearse.

Central to his dilemma was his ongoing struggle with his sexuality. He accepted the fact that he was naturally attracted to men, but he wanted desperately to lead what he viewed as a normal—i.e., heterosexual—life. "I enjoyed having sex with women, although they always complained about the size of my cock and the fact that it hurt. I remember one girl that I used to fuck, whose vagina was either so shallow or her diaphragm was so close to the edge that my dick would get about halfway in and then feel like it hit a brick wall." Eventually, he realized that he just didn't like women all that much. "The part I did not like about women was having to deal with their bitchiness, their self-centered attitudes, or having to talk to them after fucking them." This general indictment of the fairer sex stemmed in large part from Drew's early relationship with his older sister. "We never liked each other, and I felt that if she represented women as a whole, I didn't want any part of them."

Drew had reached a point at which he really needed to make a choice and get on with his life. As was often the case with him, he chose to proceed along the least conventional path. When he won the trip to New York, he was dating a very nice young woman. Her only real failing was the fact that she was female, so "she didn't have a nice big dick." Consequently, he didn't want to share this free holiday with her; unfortunately, he had no male friends he wanted to ask along either. He certainly didn't want to go alone.

In the end, he didn't ask anyone he knew at all. "This was going to be my last-ditch effort to be heterosexual, and I was determined the trip would be really interesting for me. I wanted to give the straight life one last chance." With that in mind, Drew went to the beach, set out to pick up the first beautiful blond beach bunny he could find, and tried to convince her to go with him. "Looking back, I cringe when I think about this, but at the time I had to do it. I kept thinking that only I could make my life interesting. I mean, if I didn't jerk my own dick, how would I ever hope to have an orgasm?" How, indeed?

On the day Drew decided to take his destiny in hand, the sun was shining brightly in Hermosa Beach. "I remember it was a weekday. I figured any female hanging out on the beach on a weekday obviously had no job, or she would be working at this time of day. I went for a bike ride on the strand and started looking over the crop." Drew soon spotted a very leggy blond, all by herself on a colorful beach towel. He parked his bike, mustered his courage, and sat down beside her.

She was not enchanted. Not initially, anyway. "She looked at me the way all long-legged beach bunnies look at guys that come up beside them, especially after they have gone to great lengths to find a solitary spot on the beach." However, Drew persevered and managed to pique the blond's interest with his improbable tale of free trips and game-show winnings, all hers for the asking. Although she explained that she had just returned from New York the previous week, Drew told her he didn't care. She was the one and only woman he wanted to take with him. He answered her every objection and finally convinced her to join him.

To avoid disturbing the fantasy he was already beginning to build around this young woman, Drew wanted her to remain a mystery until they were on the plane to New York. "I don't want you to think I'm strange—not that you don't already— but I'd like to make this a real trip for both of us. I don't want to know anything about you or have you know anything about me until we board the plane. That way it'll be a totally new experience for both of us. It'll be fun! The people at the travel agency told me it would take about six weeks to plan the trip, so I'll be in touch." As he walked back to retrieve his bike he was euphoric. "I had a feeling of real accomplishment. I went up to a total stranger, asked for something, and actually got it. It was the first time in my life that had happened to me."

Back at his apartment he told his roommate Tom about what he had done. Tom just shook his head and asked him how the shyest kid at Natick High had managed to pull it off. By now his fantasy was full-blown, threatening to run away with him. "I truly hoped that I had met Miss Right and that I was going to live happily ever after. I had all these visions of what the trip was going to be like. We would go to New York and fall in love. She was going to be everything a guy could hope for. Hell, maybe she even had a 12-inch clit! We stayed in touch by phone, and everything went along without a hitch. It was all just too perfect." Too perfect? Perhaps, but it turned out to be a hell of a lot of fun, expanding Drew's horizons in ways he had never imagined.

The great day finally came, and Drew boarded his flight with Ingrid, his blond fantasy woman. As they talked, Ingrid matter-of-factly told Drew that she was bisexual. Drew, somewhat shocked that his choice of female companion had lesbian tendencies, spilled the beans as well. Ingrid's facade of indifference melted at this stroke of candidness, and she adopted the role of confidante. "Don't you worry about anything, honey," she told Drew. "We're going to have ourselves a ball."

They hit the ground running. From their all-expenses-paid base at what was then the Americana Hotel, they made tracks for Greenwich Village. "Ingrid was wild. She enjoyed sex and had absolutely no inhibitions about picking guys up. The first day, Ingrid picked a guy up and took him back to the hotel. I wasn't quite so bold and ended up alone. When I went back to our room—we were sharing a hotel room, remember—she was still there with the guy. I walked right in on them. I was embarrassed as hell and started to leave, but she called me back and told me to get undressed and join them. What could I do?"

What he could do, as it turned out, was follow Ingrid's lead. Ingrid had never seen Drew naked, and when she did the wheels in her fertile imagination began to turn. "She got this wicked gleam in her eyes and informed the guy who'd been eating her out that he'd have to suck my cock if he wanted to fuck her. He wasn't any too thrilled about it, but he really wanted a piece of ass, so he agreed. I climbed into bed with them and started making out with Ingrid while her date tried to suck my cock. At the time I felt like the coolest swinger ever born."

This encounter set the tone for their entire trip. They'd go and pick up guys, gay or straight, sometimes one of each, take them back to the hotel, feed them elaborate meals compliments of *Name That Tune,* then fuck their brains out. "The bed in that hotel room saw nonstop action. Sometimes we'd each be screwing a guy, side by side. As often as not, partners would change at some point during the proceedings. It seemed that no holds were barred. Guys who had no interest in women would get turned on to me, then Ingrid would take advantage of them. There was this one guy, a really gorgeous man, whose cock would shrivel every time Ingrid got near it. She waited till I was screwing the guy, then climbed onto his dick and took a free ride. The guy practically turned inside out."

By the time the New York holiday was over Drew had reached an important decision. "I had such a great time that I decided I wanted to be gay. I no longer had any guilt over it. It was what I wanted my life to be, and I didn't give a shit who knew it. I was finally ready to live my life for me, by my own rules. The only thing I resented at first was that it had taken me so long to figure it out."

Drew didn't have much free time to resent his status as a slow learner. Within a few days of his return from New York Drew was back at Hermosa Beach. Now bereft of the blond beach-bunny fantasy that had drawn him to ask Ingrid to join him on his Big Apple jaunt, he was ready to move in another direction. All he needed was a little push.

He'd gone bicycling near the pier and had stopped to rest. His blue eyes scanned the sand but not in search of curvaceous female flesh. "I was sitting in front of a bar called Mermaid when I became aware that someone was watching me. I was in a lousy mood and didn't feel much like striking up a conversation with anyone—and then I looked at him. I remember thinking that if ever GI Joe were to come to life, this is what he would look like. My heart jerked in my chest.

"He was about 35 years old, 5 foot 10, with closely cropped hair and the bluest, most soulful eyes I had ever seen. Added to that was the fact that he had a perfect pattern of hairs on his chest. My first real fetish was body hair—I guess that guy in the hearse at Woodstock had a lasting subconscious effect on me. I stared at him and wondered how I could possibly have lived in Hermosa Beach all this time and never picked up on another guy. Now, just a few days back from New York, I was aware of every queer on the West Coast."

While Drew pondered this realignment of his sexual radar, he and the handsome stranger cruised each other. "He looked at me. I looked back at him and smiled. He looked at me again and smiled. This went on long enough for me to start feeling pretty stupid. I mean, was he going to come on to me or what?"

Drew was ready to get up and walk away when the handsome stranger finally spoke. He told Drew that he liked his hair, which Drew thought was pretty lame as pickup lines went. It did, however, make a connection that would utterly change Drew's life. As they talked Drew discovered that the man, Richard Cole, was from Maine. Their shared geographical roots gave them something to talk about, and Drew began to feel increasingly comfortable—and increasingly turned on.

When Richard told Drew that he was with the man who had been standing across from them all this time, Drew wasn't quite sure what to make of the statement. "I thought it was strange because we were talking for a long time and this other guy was just standing there across the way like we weren't even alive." Richard introduced the sullen man as Michael, and Michael fell in with them as all three walked back to smoke a joint at Richard's place. "Michael didn't have much to say, and I got the distinct feeling that he was really pissed off at Richard for inviting me along. I didn't care, because I was going to fuck with GI Joe."

Richard led him into the bedroom of his house and started to undress. He then stepped up to Drew and began groping him—and was astounded. "Richard did a double take. He hesitated, then felt around my crotch some more—more as exploration than as a sexual act." After Drew assured him that what he was feeling was all real, Richard announced, "You have a huge cock. And I should know, because I'm an expert on cocks."

Richard dropped to his knees, and Drew thought back to the days when he'd been known in school as Pony Boy. "Although I had never given much thought to the size of my dick, it seemed that lately a lot of people were noticing it and being quite vocal about it."

Richard, in the meantime, had quickly progressed beyond the verbal, although he was still being quite oral. "Richard put both hands around my dick and put the head into his mouth. It felt warm and good. Slowly he took finger after finger away until my prick was packed firmly down his throat. He held it there for what seemed to be an eternity. His eyes rolled back into his head in ecstasy as he finally came up for air. 'I could do that all day long,' he said, his voice deeper and huskier after his throat had been stretched out by my cock. He started sucking me again, and I could see Michael sitting out in the living room with his hands folded in his lap like he was sitting in church listening to a sermon."

Drew finally asked Richard what was going on with

Michael. Richard told him that if the guy was so stupid as to sit out there and sulk while in the presence of such a huge piece of meat, it was his own problem. "Richard ended his remarks by ramming my rock-hard cock all the way back down his throat again and giving me the best blow job of my life. I was amazed. Here I was, making love to this perfect fantasy of a man while his boyfriend sat in the living room, waiting for it all to be over with. Wow, gay life was the best! None of the rules seemed to apply to gay relationships that applied to straight ones—or so I thought at the time. When it was all over I made my exit, leaving them to sort things out. Although I had a great time, I never really expected to see Richard again."

A few days later the phone rang. It was a call from Richard— not to ask for a date but to inform Drew that he had given Richard the clap. Drew was mortified but, given his wild behavior in New York, he knew that anything was possible. It might even explain the sore throat he had been afflicted with, even though he had no other cold symptoms. He apologized and assured Richard that he would take care of the problem.

Several weeks passed, during which time Drew moved into an apartment on his own and started settling into the lifestyle of a single gay man. Just as he was getting comfortable, Richard called him up. Drew was surprised, figuring that after what he'd given Richard, the man would never want to see him again. Richard, however, was quite philosophical about it: It had happened to him before, and he was just glad he had been able to reach Drew and let him know what was going on. He also wanted Drew to know that Michael, the prudish boyfriend, was now history. "How would you like to go out tonight for dinner?"

"You really want to see me again?" Drew asked, amazed at this unexpected turn of events. When Richard replied in the affirmative, Drew agreed to go. They met at 8 that night and went to a fish house for a nice meal. Drew had swordfish. "When we got back to Richard's place, we smoked a joint and went into his bedroom to make love. I was feeling a little strange but attributed it to the fact that I was still new to the gay life and maybe just a little nervous over seeing such a handsome guy a second time. Then I started having a hard time breathing. My temperature started to rise, and my skin began to itch like I was getting a rash. Then my body began to swell, my nose started running, and I began sneezing uncontrollably. I had never been so sick in my whole life."

Richard diagnosed Drew's problem as a seafood allergy and insisted he stay the night just in case he began to experience difficulty breathing. "I was puffed up to twice my normal size and had a bright red rash all over my body. I was very pretty! I couldn't believe it. First, I gave the poor guy the clap, and now on our second date I was about to pull a Camille on him."

Drew did spend the night, and by the next morning his symptoms had abated. Richard left him at the house, telling him to sleep as late as he liked. Drew realized how nice the man was as he lay in his bed, staring at the ceiling. "The next day I called him back, and we tried the old dinner routine again. This time I stuck to hamburger. We went back to his place and had wild, passionate sex all night long. He seemed perfect. He did all the right things at the right time. He was 13 years my senior and had had a lot of experiences I was lacking. After sex that night, Richard admitted that he thought he was falling in love with me."

Richard Cole, the handsome GI Joe who had so dazzled Drew that day on the beach, was to have a defining influence on Drew's subsequent life and career. In contrast to the majority of gay men coming out in the mid '70s, Drew was no lone wolf content to be single and unattached. He had had enough of that as a child, living virtually alone in the family home while his parents and sister pursued their own interests. From the moment he decided he was going to live his life as an open and proud gay man, he was hardly ever alone. Ironically, Drew Okun was about as far removed temperamentally from the clone mentality, which idealized the loner, as it was possible to get.

As much mentor as lover, Richard introduced Drew to the guiltless sexual hedonism of the mid '70s, when newly liberated gays lived life without limits. In later years he provided the business acumen that made Al Parker and Surge Studio a financial success. Both men were attractive, sexually driven, and adventurous, making them an excellent match. Together they would become the perfect clone couple, joining forces to take the gay world by storm.

Drew, by his own account, also had a profound effect on Richard. "When we got together Richard was bordering on becoming just another middle-aged homosexual. His friends were suburban, boring queens whose greatest concern was when the next white sale at Bullock's would take place. Then I came along and swept him away. Not only did they think I was too young, but the fact that I became involved in pornography was too sordid for them to stomach. It wasn't long before they stopped calling, which was fine by me, because I wasn't used to or interested in the things these people found important. I would always pick a hot man over a white sale, and evidently, so would Richard."

Richard Cole's early life, as he recounted it to Drew, was an almost Dickensian tale of gloom and hardship. Cole's mother lived in abject poverty and suffered abuse at the hands of her alcoholic husband in an uninsulated shack in the Maine woods, near the town of Dixfield, notable mainly as the site of Diamond, the match and toothpick company. The company employed the town but polluted the water and fouled the air with sulfur.

On a cold November morning, after enduring a beating at the hands of her enraged spouse for failing to pay a bill on time, Richard's mother went into labor. She doubled over in pain in her sordid kitchen and saw that blood was dripping onto the floor. Realizing something was terribly wrong, she ran out of the house and went to a neighbor to summon help. On the way to the hospital the bleeding worsened and, in desperation, the neighbor went to the closest place he could think of to get help. He took Richard's mother to a nursing home that was run by Helen Cole, who had opened the home after the First World War to care for injured soldiers. By 1939 the nursing home was a success, and Helen was a respected citizen.

A baby boy was safely delivered but his mother died. When his father was called, the father's only concern was how he would be able to care for a baby. When asked what the baby's name should be he said he didn't care, just so long as he never had to see him. Helen named the baby Richard, after her late husband. With no family in sight, Helen decided to raise the baby.

Always a sickly child, Richard encountered real tragedy in the summer of 1943. An employee of the nursing home left some bleach in a cup on the back porch, and the youngster drank it. His throat was so badly burned that scar tissue formed, and once a week for the next 14 years he went to the hospital to have his throat stretched so that he could swallow. He made a game of it, always encouraging his therapist to push the rod further and further down his throat. Much to the delight of Drew and scores of other men, Richard had absolutely no gag reflex in later life.

After finishing high school and a four-year stint in the Air Force, Richard made his way to California. By that time he had figured out that he was gay. He had been involved in two long-term relationships and was on his way to middle-aged boredom when he ran into Drew on the beach.

Drew was reluctant to get involved in a relationship when they first met. He felt Richard had had so many more experiences and worried that he still had all those things to do himself. He and Richard had seen each other only three times, and Drew wasn't really sure he even wanted a lover. In fact, he still wasn't totally sure he was really gay.

Richard countered every argument, offering Drew nothing but fun, support, and freedom. He suggested that they try and see what they could work out. When Drew said he wanted the freedom to go out and meet other people, Richard told him he wasn't the jealous type. "He told me that if I went out and found someone I liked more than I liked him, then I should definitely be with that person. I couldn't believe the guy. He was so supremely self-confident. I mean, he was just too perfect."

CHAPTER SEVEN

A Deal With the Devil

Drew moved into Richard's beach house, and the two men set up housekeeping. After they had been together about two months Drew stumbled across a book that would test the flexibility of their open relationship. In one of those moments that he often referred to as life-changing, he picked up a book on the way to the toilet one morning. "You might think a book that would change someone's life would be some heavy philosophical treatise by Sartre or Aristotle or someone like that. Actually, the book that changed my life was *The Happy Hustler* by a writer named Michael Kearns. I had found it while in a crazy dash to the toilet, looking for something to read while taking a shit."

Kearns was a writer-performer pursuing a career on the stage. In a nice, ironic twist, his turn as author was merely one of his many roles. He was hired by the man who wrote the book to pose as its autobiographical subject. *Making Love* told of Kearns's alleged adventures as a hustler, which were many, varied, and lucrative. All questions of authorship aside, Drew was very impressed. "He talked about some of the scams he ran while he was a hustler, like selling used jockstraps through the mail. He also talked about hooking and dealing with pimps. I found the book utterly amazing and sat on the toilet until I finished it. By the time I was done my legs were numb and I had a huge toilet welt on my ass, but I was convinced that I was going to try being a male hooker. I mean, just once, to see what it was like."

He spent the afternoon agonizing about how to tell Richard of his plans. Although he figured it would be a good test of the openness of their open relationship, he was apprehensive. When Richard got home that evening Drew mentioned the book and floated the idea of trying his luck at hustling. As was often the case, Richard's reaction amazed the relatively innocent Drew. "He thought it would be good for me, much to my surprise. He even gave me the number of a guy he knew who could arrange things. I pretended the whole thing was a joke, but while Richard was at the store I made the call and was told that I could meet with some guy named Harry the next day in West Hollywood. I wrote down the address and stuffed it in my wallet. I don't think I slept at all that night."

Harry lived in a small, run-down bungalow—complete with a battered '56 Thunderbird parked out front—on Westbourne Drive in West Hollywood, just off La Cienega Boulevard. Drew rang the bell, and a good-looking young guy answered the door. "I went in and was led to a couch in a seedy living room. The guy—he was a stud—told me he would tell Harry that I was there." Drew cooled his heels, examining the water-stained ceiling until Harry appeared.

Harry wasn't a particularly prepossessing specimen. "Harry

was about five-six, with greasy hair combed over a huge bald spot. He was wearing an old, sweat-stained T-shirt and madras plaid Bermuda shorts. The ensemble was rounded out with dark socks and penny loafers." Harry dismissed the good-looking guy who had ushered Drew into the house and turned to check out the new talent.

"So, you want to be a hustler," Harry said, his beady eyes slithering up and down Drew's frame. "What makes you think you could be a good one?" Drew replied that he was hung like a horse and figured he could make some money with his cock. "I couldn't believe I was actually saying this. It was just like in that book I'd been reading. It was kind of exciting."

Harry asked to see Drew's cock, and Drew obliged. "I got up off the couch and reached for my crotch. I rubbed it a few times and started getting hard. I could see Harry's interest rising as the bulge in my jeans grew larger and larger. It was clear that he wanted to see more. I unbuttoned my jeans and reached in to pull out my swollen cock. It sort of got stuck down in the leg of my pants and when it finally pulled free, Harry was very impressed.

" 'Jesus! It is big! It's not often someone your height has such a big dick. Come closer,' " Drew recalled Harry as saying. "He examined my cock up close, holding it in his quivering hands. He commented on how veiny it was, practically drooling on it. Then he let it go, jerking his hands back like he'd been fondling the forbidden fruit or something. He told me to go into one of the bedrooms. He was going to call one of his clients who would rate me and judge whether I would be a good hustler or not. I wondered what the hell I was doing!

"Harry told me the client he had in mind was a famous actor. His name was Tom Ewell. He had costarred with Marilyn Monroe in Billy Wilder's film *The Seven Year Itch*. I remembered the scene where she stands on the subway grating and the wind blows her dress up. Ewell was the middle-aged guy in the suit with a real '50s-style hat who ogled her when her underwear was showing. Yeah, I knew who Tom Ewell was, but I couldn't believe he was gay.

"While I waited for Mr. Ewell to arrive, Harry showed me an old, scratched, and grainy eight-millimeter Falcon loop of hot guys sucking each other off. While I was watching this guy trying to cram a huge cock down his throat, the bedroom door opened, and in walked Tom Ewell. Honest to God, he should've been wheeled in. The guy was ancient! He had a cane and had to be helped into the room. I remember thinking that if I could do it with this guy, I could do it with anyone. As old Tom got closer and closer all I could see were those big, liver-spotted lips coming at me. I shrank back in horror. *The Happy Hustler* didn't have a chapter to cover this! There was no way I was going to be able to pull this off. I just kept thinking of the day at Hefner's when I saw Linda Lovelace waiting for that big dog. I got up and left the room."

Before Drew made good on his escape he was accosted by Harry again. The man told Drew that he knew a photographer who might be interested in taking some pictures. This was not just any photographer—this man happened to be the owner of Colt Studio. Harry asked Drew if he had ever heard of Colt. Memories of ordering photos from Colt Studio when he was in high school came flooding back to him. Drew nodded, and Harry told him to hang around.

"Harry got rid of Tom Ewell, and a few minutes later the door opened again, and Rip Colt walked into the room. He was not even vaguely what I had expected." Instead of the tall, muscular man with piercing eyes and close-cropped hair that Drew had fantasized, Colt was "heavy, wore shorts, and carried what, for lack of another word, I'd have to call a purse." After Drew provided a quick sketch of his background, Colt left the room, telling Drew to call "when you've gotten it hard."

Drew quickly called Colt back into the bedroom. Colt was clearly impressed with Drew's cock and suggested doing some test shots the following Saturday. He handed Drew his card and offered to pay him $50 for his time. Drew accepted readily. "I was very flattered. Colt Studio personified everything that was masculine, and the thought that I passed muster with Rip Colt was a real ego boost. Deep down, I hoped I'd be able to meet some of the guys I'd jerked off over when I was in high school."

Colt departed, leaving Drew to mull over the events of the day. "Perhaps I wasn't meant to be a call boy. I really hated the experience I had just had. There wasn't anything glamorous or sexy about it." Although Drew hustled throughout his career, he was never enthusiastic about it. According to journalist-illustrator Robert Richards, who interviewed Drew many times and became a close personal friend, "Drew hustled because it was expected of him as a sexual icon. He demanded outrageous amounts of money and, if the client was willing to pay, he would do it."

Colt Studio, on the other hand, had all the glamour and sex appeal that any man could handle. "Only hot guys worked for Colt, and that's the kind of men I wanted to meet. I wondered how Richard would react to this new turn of events."

Drew had sneaked off to his little adventure that day without bothering to tell Richard. He really didn't expect the episode to amount to more than an inconsequential lark. After his experience, "the very idea of wanting to hustle was embarrassing. I mean, anyone who could read such a silly book and then try to actualize some of the author's wild scams would have to be right out of *I Love Lucy.*" He was, however, apprehensive about Richard's reaction to the news that he had the opportunity to work for Colt Studios. "I know that if someone I was going out with was in a position to get it on with every hunk in Hollywood and asked for my permission, I would've said no."

When Drew got back from his interview Richard was already at home. When asked about his day, Drew casually mentioned that he had been interviewed by the guy who owned Colt Studio and that he had an appointment to be photographed. Richard was elated, much to Drew's surprise. "He thought it was a great opportunity for me to meet some really hot guys. His only request was that I share the wealth with him." Drew had put his new lover's talk of an open relationship to the test, and Richard had been true to his word. "He wasn't going to put restrictions on me as far as allowing me to experience new and interesting things. This was to become the most basic underpinning of our relationship, and this is why it was able to endure for all those years."

By the time Saturday rolled around, Drew was a bundle of nerves. All of a sudden the idea of taking off his clothes and having his picture taken by a total stranger seemed a little intimidating. What if he didn't photograph well? What if he couldn't get an erection?

Drew set off early to find Colt's house in the Hollywood hills. When he pulled up in front of the large, stucco house, "it looked very froufrou-queerish to me. It was exactly what I expected." He walked up to the front door, knocked, and was buzzed inside. "The house was actually very nice. I was greeted by Rip Colt himself."

Shortly after Drew's arrival they went into Colt's photography studio and went to work. "I can distinctly remember him sitting down with me before we started and asking if I really wanted to do this. He told me I was about to stand in front of a camera that had the potential to change my life, and that once I had done it there would be no turning back. This made me even more nervous than I already was. I could never have believed how true those words would turn out to be." Drew's decision to live as a gay man was about to become spectacularly public.

Drew finally announced that he was as ready as he'd ever be, and the shoot began. "Colt held up the camera, focused, and shot the first picture. The click of the shutter seemed to echo in my head. I actually got a rush from it of the kind you get when you take a hit of poppers."

The shoot went well. Colt knew exactly what he wanted and Drew was able to give it to him. "I had seen several of the girls being photographed at the Playboy mansion, so I just did what I remembered seeing them do, which was basically moving a little bit after each shot so that each photo would be a little different from the one before. Rip seemed quite pleased with me. He was very patient, giving me plenty of time to get aroused and in the mood.

"I kept waiting for him to put the make on me—you know, offer to help me get it up. I learned very quickly that he makes love to you with his camera without ever even touching you. The man is really an artist. He was able to make me look like someone I was not. When I saw the photographs I had to study them to make sure they were really of me."

One of the things Drew learned that day was just how tedious it was to be a model. The session went on for several hours and was exhausting. "I had to hold very uncomfortable positions, always keeping an erection. I had no idea that in order to get a good picture I'd have to go through such contortions. All in all, modeling was much more difficult than I had imagined it would be. Still, I knew the photos would be around for a long time, and I was determined to do the best job I could. I felt like my ass was literally on the line."

When the session finally ended, Drew was asked to sign a model release, giving Colt the right to use the pictures as he saw fit. Until that point Drew had felt that he was basically in charge of the situation. The stroke of a pen, he realized, would change that. "I think it was the first time I realized how important my signature was on a piece of paper. I felt a little lightheaded as I signed the release. Then it was done, and there was no turning back. I saw a slight smile flicker over Colt's face, like maybe I had just sold my soul or something."

CHAPTER EIGHT

Introducing Al Parker

Drew didn't have to wait long before he could satisfy his curiosity about this photo session. Colt called him a couple of weeks later and requested another shoot. Then more shoots were scheduled, and Drew knew he had made a good impression. Drew still didn't have a clue about how he looked in any of these photographs, because Colt worked slowly in developing and printing his work. All he heard was that the photos were good and that he would like them. As a longtime Colt fan, Drew could hardly suppress his excitement. "I felt very lucky that Rip was the first photographer I dealt with, because Colt Studio was considered to be the best in the business. Luckily, since I started at the top, there are no pictures of me sitting in a seedy hotel room, with a rate card tacked on the door in the background, wearing a Mexican sombrero and an embarrassed expression."

After several long posing sessions Drew knew Colt would be using his photos commercially, so he asked him about choosing a pseudonym. Without even looking up from the camera he was adjusting Colt told Drew that it was all settled: He was going to be "Al Parker." Drew was dismayed. " 'Al Parker'? Isn't that a really boring, forgettable name? I was hoping for something a little more exotic. 'Al Parker' is so Waspy and bland." Colt stood firm, telling him the name couldn't be changed because the captioned photos had already gone to the printer. Colt added that he often named his models after famous people in the entertainment business. "Just be glad I didn't call you Yehudi Menuhin," he quipped, referring to the famous violinist.

Years later Drew told Robert Richards in an interview that he had never warmed up to the name. "It sounded so very forgettable, but it went into print, and suddenly everyone knew me as 'Al.' I don't really mind anymore, but I do wonder what it stands for—Alexander? Alan?" In an aside that Richards chose not to make public at the time, Drew lowered his voice and suggested a third possibility. "Alice?"

Bland or not, Al Parker quickly became all the things that Drew Okun was not. He became the *other,* the alter ego who could get away with things Drew only dreamed of doing. "In my life I have found that as Al Parker I can do nothing wrong. I can get away with anything, and I'm very successful. In real life, on the other hand, I rarely do anything right." No wonder he was so often willing to let Al take center stage.

Drew was soon way too busy to waste time brooding over his disappointing new moniker. He had photo shoots lined up, there were films in the works, and besides, "I was sure I would do this a couple more times, the results would be released, and [they] would quickly sink to the bottom of the porno pile with all the other stuff that was being released. I never thought it was going to be a career. I always felt it would be good training for being in the film industry. If you are a director, say, and you have never been an actor, you can't expect to get a good performance out of people, because you can't relate to the way they feel in front of the camera. I was convinced that if I could go in front of a camera, take off all my clothes, and perform, then I could be asked to play the part of Bozo the Clown and not bat an eye. I looked at this whole experience as a learning process. I never in my wildest dreams thought that what I was doing would make a difference in my life."

Three months passed before Drew's pictures appeared in print. Colt told him his nude debut would be in a new magazine called *Mandate.* "He told me I was going to be on the cover. Richard and I were very excited about this. There was absolutely no jealousy on his part. As a matter of fact, I think he was more excited than I was, just thinking about the fact that his lover was going to be on the cover of a magazine."

In the meantime, Colt kept Drew busy. After several solo shoots, he decided to team Drew up with Bob Bishop, another newcomer to the scene. "He showed me a photo of him and asked me if I liked him. Bob was blond, with a great smile, a huge muscular chest, and a belly with enough ridges on it to do a week's worth of laundry." Arrangements were made to spend a weekend shooting still photographs out in the desert. Colt even offered to let Richard come along if he'd agree to act as his assistant. "Richard couldn't believe his ears when I told him about it. The thought of going on a Colt shoot was every gay guy's fantasy!"

To make the weekend even more fantasy-perfect, Drew was notified that the *Mandate* spread was put together, so he could drop by the magazine's office on Sunset Boulevard and pick up a copy on his way out of town. "The pictures were incredible. I had to look twice to make sure they were of me! I remembered the shoot and had to laugh. We'd driven out into the Mojave Desert, bouncing along in Rip's Blazer. He'd seen an abandoned boxcar on a siding, and we stopped. He asked me to lean up against the boxcar when I got a hard-on. The photo looked great, but the intense look he had captured was really the instant I put my bare butt against the freezing cold train car. Rip could make it all look like art. I mean, he made me look great! I was very pleased, to say the least."

Rip, his assistant Bill, his newly recruited "assistant" Richard, Bob Bishop, and Drew piled into the Blazer and Richard's new camper, and set off into the Mojave. Along the way, Rip complained about how it was getting tough to find unpopulated areas where you could do a nude photo shoot in private. His words were soon to prove a colossal understatement.

"We drove for about six hours out into the hot dunes of the Mojave. After what seemed an eternity we found the ruins of an abandoned house. It had been trashed, and debris was spread all around the area. We stopped because the old house had great windows. Rip liked to use window frames as a backdrop, especially when they were nicely weathered. There was also sufficient shelter to make the area suitable as a campsite.

"The sun was just dipping down in the west, providing perfect light to shoot by. Rip took some pictures of Bob in the windows and decided to call it a day. Richard was having the time of his life, helping with the equipment and acting as a fluffer for Bob when the need arose." (A "fluffer" is the person who helps porn stars achieve and maintain erections between photos or scenes in a video shoot.) Richard was a natural for this task, which he approached with gusto.

After the equipment had been stowed, Rip Colt announced that he was going to prepare supper for the crew. He was a gourmet cook who wasn't going to let something so mundane as a Coleman stove in the middle of the desert stand between his entourage and a decent meal. "I asked what was on the menu, and he casually said, 'Pheasant under glass, rice pilaf, fresh asparagus, and for dessert, a special pudding.' Richard and I watched in disbelief as he set about preparing the food."

Bill had brought along some magic mushrooms, and Drew was able to contribute a joint. Everyone but Rip indulged in the illicit treat and settled back to relax before eating. "Richard and Bob were behind a rock, Richard working Bob's nipples and the expanse of chest that separated them. I was delighted that he was having a good time, knowing I would be able to have my turn the next morning when we did the shoot."

Then, just as the dusk faded into night and Colt prepared to serve his feast, trouble started. "We could see headlights on the horizon. Soon we realized that the headlights were coming directly toward us. By this time the drugs had kicked in, and we were all either feeling no pain or becoming extremely paranoid. I was the paranoid one. Here we were, in the middle of nowhere, nobody knew where we were, we had a new truck that didn't even have license plates yet, and we had about $25,000 worth of camera equipment piled around us. If these were desert bandits, we could be killed and buried, and nobody would ever find the bodies. As the only one who hadn't done any drugs, Rip told us to keep our cool and let him do the talking. *Great*, I thought, *on top of all this, they're going to find out we're queers.* Visions of Ned Beatty in *Deliverance* ran through my head. I practiced my pig squeals as they approached."

As the caravan came over the hill, raising a huge cloud of dust in its wake, Drew started counting headlights and realized there were at least 15 cars coming at them. "It occurred to me that an entire town must be on the move. Soon the first of the cars was upon us. The driver hit the brakes, and the battered '63 Chevy slid sideways, throwing gravel and sand as it came to a stop right in front of Rip. The passenger door flew open, and suddenly a double-barreled shotgun was staring the King of the Queers in the face."

A man called out, telling them not to move. The other cars pulled up, and door after door opened, each one sprouting a shotgun—all aimed at the hapless group of stoners. The first man, who seemed to be the leader, accused Rip and his cohorts of dismantling the abandoned house and spiriting away the materials to someplace "over the hill." He exclaimed that they were all caught in the act. The rest of the posse began shouting and laughing in a most unfriendly manner.

Colt remained unflappable. He assured the men that he and his group had only arrived that day and had not touched a thing. All they wanted to do was have a bite to eat and get a good night's sleep. The heavily armed crew didn't appear convinced, so Colt played the well-brought-up gay man's trump card—he invited the whole bunch to dinner. "The ringleader, a crusty old coot, exchanged glances with his cohorts, trying to decide what to do," Drew recalled. "Finally, with a sideways squint, he lowered his gun. The others followed suit, and you could hear the hammers uncocking in the dry desert air.

"Then they began to get out of their cars and trucks, circling around us warily. Some of them were extremely hot in a scruffy sort of way. There was one man who was obviously there with his son. The kid was about 14, just bordering on manhood. Believe me, I would've done it with him in a hot second! The drugs had really started hitting their peak, and it was taking all my concentration just to stay on my feet. I shot a look at Richard, who just stood there looking like the Marlboro Man, his beautiful hair blowing in the wind. He caught my eye and winked back in a reassuring way that let me know he thought we were going to be OK."

Convinced that Drew and company presented no threat, the visiting men decided to stay the night as well so that the following morning they could ambush the man who'd been stealing the house. "Then we'll have us a *real* shoot-out," they said. The old coot, so the tale went, had just finished building his home when the neighbor on the next hill decided to remodel his own place. In order to save money he just came over and helped himself to whatever he wanted, leaving the old coot's house in its present state of disassembly. The group sympathized with the coot, and they all sat down to eat.

Colt wisely simplified his menu to chicken 'n' rice and began to dole it out. Food for five didn't go far among 20 men, but after the mushrooms Drew and his pals weren't really hungry. Their uninvited guests were more interested in the liquor they had brought to fortify themselves when they had been convinced they were on their way to a range war, so all food shortages were easily forgiven. Once they had cleaned up, Colt and his crew announced that they were going to bed because they had a long drive ahead of them the next morning.

"Satisfied that we weren't a threat, the old coot and the others bid us a good night. Just about the time we had settled into our sleeping bags in the camper, we heard the first shots. The men had been putting away the booze for at least two hours, and now they were taking the empties and setting them up for target practice. I don't know whether it was the liquor or what, but these guys were not good shots. Pretty soon, Richard and I could tell that all the shots weren't going in the direction where the targets had been set up. The men were getting louder and more rowdy as the minutes went by. I was absolutely convinced they were going to shoot us, bury us in the sand, and make off with our new rig.

"The shooting got wilder and wilder, as the guys began taking potshots at anything they could focus on. I could hear one of them puking near the back of our truck and thought how strange it was that all of this violence was taking place so far away from the city. Here we were, deep in the desert, miles from anything, and the air was so heavy with lead, it wasn't safe to raise our heads.

"Just when we thought we were going to lose it, the shooting stopped. All the men got quiet and began drifting toward the campfire, spent—as if they had had a communal orgasm. They all sat down and stared into the fire. The vent in the top of our truck above the sleeping area was open, and the voices of the men drifted into the truck. At first it was nothing more than a jumble of sounds, but then Richard and I simultaneously zeroed in on the conversation taking place just outside.

"The voice of the handsome youngster I'd noticed earlier rose above the others and silenced them as he began talking. 'You know what I like best about jerking off, Dad?' he asked. 'I like how you can just whip it out and beat on it. It gets all hard and then you shoot your load and it just feels so good.' The other men remained silent, listening, captivated by the image of what the boy was describing. I was peering out the window, wondering what would happen next. Then the father looked at his son and spoke to him. 'Boy,' he said slowly and meaningfully, his strong voice trailing off into silence for a while. 'Sometimes I think you're a goddamn queer!' The father then began to laugh and slapped his son on the back, knocking him off the log. The other men joined in the laughter, and so did the son. It was one of the hottest father-son moments I could ever have imagined.

"By now Richard and I both had raging hard-ons. He slowly pushed himself down to my crotch and swallowed my cock. I was still looking out the window at the men around the fire. If they had ever figured out what was going on in the truck, I wonder if they would've killed us or joined in. I fantasized on the latter. Richard and I made love for hours while listening to each man around the campfire regale the youngster with tales of the first time he jerked off. Each story was hotter than the next. Richard and I came multiple times, then drifted off to sleep, lulled by the voices of the men.

"Just before dawn I woke up and heard Rip moving around outside, preparing to make a getaway before our rowdy pals woke up. We timed our departure, turning the keys of our trucks simultaneously. Slowly, without revving the engines, we made our stealthy departure across the cool desert sands."

CHAPTER NINE

Fame, No Fortune

The photos Rip Colt had taken received a remarkable amount of exposure. The male skin magazine business was just coming into its own, and newcomers like *Honcho* and *Mandate* were begging for photos of hot models. Photographers, Rip Colt among them, were trading photographs for ad space, and before long Drew's nude photos were turning up everywhere. "I was happy about it because every picture was a good one."

What Drew was not so happy about was the manner in which Colt introduced him to the public. Models were promoted by means of a brochure sent out to Colt Studio's mailing list. These brochures celebrated the masculinity, virility, and desirability of a model, exhorting recipients to pony up the cash for a set of hot photos. Drew's brochure, in sharp contrast, was couched in the form of an apology. "I was eagerly awaiting the first Colt brochure that featured my photographs. I was very disappointed when I saw it. Although Rip admitted that my dick was on a par with Toby's—my own hero from the days when I jacked off over him in high school—he more or less apologized in advance for my body, which wasn't up to Colt's usual standards. He went on to say that while I wasn't as well defined as most Colt models, my big dick made up for that. He ended by saying that people might eventually get over my body. I 'might grow on them,' was the way he put it." Drew got his revenge by becoming the biggest moneymaker Colt had ever had, although it was a hollow victory.

Drew's photos made the rounds in the burgeoning gay-porn industry. Brentwood Studios, a pioneer in the X-rated gay-film business, had a number of young directors on the payroll, cranking out short silent films of hot guys getting it on singly, in pairs, and in groups. One of the best was Matt Sterling. In 1976 Sterling was still a relative unknown churning out above-average eight-millimeter sex loops for the Brentwood assembly line. A loop is a single reel of eight-millimeter film usually lasting 12 to 15 minutes and containing one sex scene, start to finish. The majority of early gay films were composed of loops—some linked by common settings or performers, others assembled in a totally random fashion. A few directors were producing explicit gay feature films with distinct plots, but the majority of footage released in these early years was in the form of eight-millimeter loops.

Drew was signed by Brentwood and, coupled with director Sterling, he made his film debut in the seafarer epic *Challenger*. Al—for simplicity, I will refer to Drew by his professional name when discussing his films—is paired with two slim, boyish types. (This is, by the way, the one and only time Al Parker appears in a film or on video without a beard. Drew was convinced his chin was weak and kept it hidden under whiskers for the rest of his life.) The threesome romped on a large sailboat, sucking and fucking their way to multiple orgasms. The film, in the colorful words of one reviewer, offered "a raunchy group of men having sex like pigs!" Al's nascent star quality was clearly in evidence as he exhibited his legendary prowess for the first time.

This first venture into the world of gay porn was almost his last. "The experience of making *Challenger* was so bad and so negative, especially in regard to the amount of time it took to film it and the conditions it was filmed under, that I really never wanted to do it again. I wanted to have a good time. If having sex isn't fun when you're doing it, I don't want to do it. I didn't need the money that badly. I was into making porn for the fun of it."

On the other hand, the men in the Colt films "looked like they were having a really good time. I wanted to join them." Drew may have been irritated by Colt's less-than-gallant disclaimer in the promotional brochure, but he was too smart to let himself be cut off from such a resource by a fit of pique. Colt was understandably pleased by the public's reaction to his newest sensation and continued to use Drew as a model. Drew, for his part, was more than happy to be used, especially if being used included working with some of the men who had featured so prominently in his adolescent wet dreams.

Colt gave Drew free rein to choose the person he would costar with in his Colt film debut. Drew, understandably, was delighted. "It didn't take me any time at all to think about it. I wanted to work with Toby, the hot stud who had turned me on so much in high school. All I could think of was that picture of his big, uncut dick next to the Coke can. Rip said he would try to contact him and see if he would be interested in meeting me. I could hardly wait to find out if I turned him on as much as he did me."

Colt called back a few days later with the good news: Toby

did indeed want to work with Drew. The only potential obstacle was Richard. In the early days of their relationship Drew was still somewhat apprehensive regarding his new lover's reaction to these very public sexual trysts.

He needn't have worried. The ever-tolerant Richard was almost as excited as Drew at the prospect of meeting Toby. The mundane suburban existence of a middle-aged gay man that had been looming before he connected with Drew was rapidly receding into the distant might-have-been. Besides, as he reminded Drew, they could use the 100 bucks Drew would be paid for his costarring role.

Everything was arranged. Toby would meet Rip, Drew, and Richard near Palm Springs at a house in the desert. Rip picked up Drew and Richard in the city and ferried them to their destination. "The ride seemed to take forever, and I wondered what kind of person Toby was going to be. Rip never told you too much about who you would work with, nor did he ever let any meeting take place prior to the shoot. He wanted everything on film, from the initial chemistry to the final money shot. Everything had to be spontaneous and unrehearsed." On the way to the rendezvous point Drew asked Rip what the premise of this new epic was going to be. Rip just smiled and showed him the single prop he had brought—a parachute.

When the meeting took place, Drew was thoroughly impressed. "We got to the house, a big modern affair that was still under construction, and Toby came out to meet us. He was a lot more sophisticated than I had thought he would be. He was British, and he had an accent. He was the lover of a very important film producer, and they had been together for years. He was a world traveler. He had been everywhere and seen everything."

Toby worked exclusively—and infrequently—for Colt. It

was quite obvious to Drew that Toby was turned on to him, and it temporarily unnerved him. Fortunately, during their introductory conversation one of Drew's nonsexual passions was mentioned. "It came out that he was a big backgammon fan. I had played lots of backgammon at the Playboy mansion, and when Toby claimed I could never beat him, I took up the challenge."

When they arrived at the site Colt had chosen for the shoot, Toby and Drew faced off across the board while Richard helped Rip get the equipment ready. "We played a game; I beat him. I think he was genuinely surprised, and he began to take me more seriously. My nervousness melted away, and I was able to approach him man to man."

Typically enough, there was no script for the proposed film. All Colt had was the parachute and nothing else. They were in the middle of a perfectly flat desert, and there was no way to put the chute into play, short of having Toby jump out of an airplane. At that juncture, Drew's ingenuity and sense of humor came into play. "Far off in the distance there was a lone tree sticking up out of the sand. I thought it would be funny to have Toby get stuck in the only tree in the entire desert, then have me drive by, spot him, and rescue him." Colt saw the humor in it as well, so they drove over to the tree and set up the defining shot of the film loop eventually sold to the viewing public as *Chute*.

As the moment approached, Drew's nerves returned, churning his stomach and making him fear that he wouldn't be able to get it up. He had had sex with any number of men by this point, and he was mad about the sexy lover who backed him 100% in this new venture, but he was still in awe of the situation. "This would be the first time that I would have sex with someone I regarded as a sexual hero. I was more turned on than

I had ever been. I had lusted after this guy since I was a young-ster, and now I was going to have him. It was the first time in my life that I felt I had set a situation into motion that was actually going to come to fruition. I mean, I initially set out to do modeling so that I would be able to have sex with this guy, and today it was really going to happen."

Colt began the shoot by taking still photographs that could be used for promotion and magazine sales. The two men stood side by side, and the chemistry was undeniable. "I had an instant hard-on, and Toby wasn't far behind. I was delighted to notice that my equipment stood up nicely to my idol's." It went so well that the still shots were quickly finished, and they took a break. Drew won another game of backgammon, and Toby swore to have his revenge.

The actual filming was more fun than Drew had dared to imagine. "It seemed that as fast as Rip could load the film in the camera it would be gone, and he'd have to tell us to stop while he loaded more. Film comes in rolls of 400 feet, and it goes through the camera at an alarming rate. Reloading is a tedious, time-consuming task, and when the camera would stop, we weren't always able to. Some of the very best stuff would happen while the film was being reloaded. Toby and I were going to town, and between shots Richard was able to join in, helping to keep us both fluffed. I had realized that a happy lover is a permissive lover, so I more or less let Richard take over. I figured that as long as everyone was having fun, things would go smoothly." It was a theory that proved itself valid over the course of the next dozen years.

During one of the breaks for reloading film, Drew got another inspiration that contributed to making *Chute* such a memorable little jewel of a film. "It was getting very hot, and it wasn't long before we broke out some beer. I poured some of it on Toby's cock, and Richard and I took turns licking it off. Rip happened to see this and asked if I could do it for the camera. Before long Richard's brand-new truck was awash in beer. I could see him wincing every time we sloshed the smelly liquid on the truck's interior, but it was all in the name of art. It was the hottest thing that ever happened in that truck."

Chute remains a classic—the passage of time has done nothing to diminish its impact. As the film opens, Toby is hanging in a solitary tree out in the middle of nowhere. Al just happens to drive by and see him. This moment represents the culmination of Drew's most cherished boyhood fantasy, and it shows. He ogles Toby like he just might be a misplaced Christmas stocking. A heartbeat later he scurries up the tree to the rescue.

When Drew revives his prize, the first thing Toby grabs is Al's basket, hauling our hero's dick out into the open. Still aloft, they help one another strip. The men are beautifully matched—both hung, both sleekly muscled. Drew, in his role as Al Parker, soon-to-be-major sexual icon, is startlingly handsome. Everything about Al Parker—the lean, subtly sculpted body; the luminous skin; the handsome face; the impish, playful expression; the voracious sensuality—demands the viewer's attention.

There is never a moment's doubt that Al is completely into the scene—he is the consummate sexual animal. He worships Toby's big, uncut cock, sucking it like he means it. How many of us, after all, can conjure our sex partners from the pages of magazines—and get paid for doing it? The loop resonates with authenticity. Toby does justice to Al as well, clearly turned on by his young acolyte.

The beer scene comes across beautifully on film. As the Heineken begins to flow, it is clear that both men are having a great time. Toby bathes Al's hairy hole with beer, then finger-fucks him, really working him over. An apprehensive Al looks over his shoulder at Toby's massive, hooded cock as it angles high in the air, but there is no penetration. Toby comes and Al eats it, then they kiss. As the loop closes, the two men drive off into the desert.

Chute remained one of Drew's favorite films. "Looking at that film, it is obvious that I was having the time of my life. It was the first time I realized that dreams actually do come true. I can only hope this is how models felt when they were about to work with me for the first time."

Once his pictures began appearing in the skin mags, Al Parker—much to Drew Okun's surprise and delight—became a phenomenon. "I started turning up in all the magazines. I was amazed at how many people were seeing the pictures. Before long I was being recognized in supermarkets and department stores. People were coming up to me on the street and asking if I was Al Parker. They didn't know Drew Okun from Adam, but they knew all about Al Parker and his big dick."

Naturally, the attention stroked his ego, although he strove to keep it all in perspective. "I knew that the worst thing a public person could ever do was to believe his own publicity. I just got lucky and happened to be in the right place at the right time. It was all very flattering and, at least at the beginning, a lot of fun. Fortunately for me, Richard was loving it as much as I was."

Drew soon learned that there were other ways to profit from his status as a Colt model. Although he had been less than enchanted by his brief encounter with Tom Ewell, he was still interested when Rip Colt called him up one day to ask whether he would be interested in meeting a legendary Hollywood director. Drew's autobiographical notes don't specifically mention any exchange of cash for services, but the context makes it clear that the meeting Colt arranged between him and George Cukor was intended for more than just conversation.

Cukor, famous for directing Hollywood screen goddesses Joan Crawford and Katherine Hepburn—and infamous for being fired as the director of *Gone With the Wind* when Clark Gable refused to be directed by a "goddamned fairy"—was in his 70s when Drew first encountered him. His homosexuality was an open secret in Hollywood, as was his propensity for handsome young men. Colt had a stable of such young men, so the connection between the two was logical, if not obvious.

"One day Rip asked me if I would be interested in meeting an old Hollywood director. Rip said he didn't make these kinds of arrangements often, but seeing that I had a genuine interest in film, he was willing to make an exception." If Drew took this disclaimer at face value, he could claim nothing but naïveté. He did have a legitimate interest in filmmaking, and Cukor had coaxed more Oscar-winning performances out of his stars than any other director.

Drew arrived at Cukor's mansion in his most recent vehicle, a yellow bread truck, and parked in the circular drive. There were three houses in the compound—the other two were rented by Katherine Hepburn and her lover, Spencer Tracy. "Walking onto the compound was like stepping into a time warp. The buildings were like miniature White Houses, complete with columns and ornate windows. The courtyard was dominated by a swimming pool flanked by beautiful gardens."

The interior was no less a revelation, beginning with its copper-ceilinged foyer and the bronze bust of Tallulah Bankhead. "I had never seen such a beautiful home. George obviously had impeccable taste." As Drew contemplated the beauty around him, and the fame of its owner, George Cukor entered the room. "I was seated in the living room when he entered. He was about five-seven tall, had a couple of wisps of hair on his head, and very large lips. I'm sure he could have been attractive at one time in his life, but he reminded me of an older version of Don Knotts. He was even older than Tom Ewell, which qualified him as the oldest homosexual I had ever met."

Drew was distinctly ill at ease. "I realized that he was a legend who had seen and done everything, and I was some young piece of meat conjured up for an afternoon's entertainment. Maybe he was expecting me to be just another hustler, but before long we were engaged in an intelligent conversation. He started to tell me these fabulous old Hollywood stories, dishing the dirt on stars of the past. One of the more interesting stories he told was of how he was in the middle of directing Marilyn Monroe in *Something's Got to Give* when she died. He gave me the feeling that he thought she had been a murder victim, not a suicide."

As the old man spun his tales, lunch was announced. "A servant came in and told us that lunch was ready in the dining room. Two white-coated men were there to wait on us—one for George, and one for me. George sat at one end of the table, and I sat at the other, which seemed like it was about a hundred miles distant. There was a huge flower arrangement in the middle that you had to talk around.

"I was all prepared for a gourmet extravaganza. The two servants reappeared, pushing matching dinner carts with huge silver dome lids on them. Moving with the precision of ballet dancers, the servants pushed the carts across the room, arriving at opposite ends of the table simultaneously. A crystal bowl with an orchid in it was placed in front of me. I didn't know whether to eat it or what, so I decided to wait and see what George did with his. Good thing I waited—it was a finger bowl. After delicately dipping his fingertips in the water, he motioned to the servants. They removed the lids with a flourish to reveal a fine china plate with two boiled hot dogs on it, topped with a pair of fried eggs. There wasn't even a sprig of parsley for garnish. It was the strangest meal ever served to me."

After successfully negotiating the perils of lunch—do you dip the wienie in the egg yolk?—the pair retired to another sitting room and continued to talk. Cukor asked Drew what aspect of filmmaking interested him, and Drew told him that he wanted to be a producer. Cukor encouraged him, suggesting that producing (unlike directing, set decoration, or lighting) couldn't be taught. "He told me anything was possible, so I should just go out and do it."

After that little tidbit of advice the mood changed. Cukor hit a button beside his chair, and every door and window in the place locked with a resounding click. "He reached for the lamp switch and turned the lights down low. All I can remember are those liver-spotted lips coming at me. It was like I was looking through a convex mirror, one where the nose looked all enlarged, taking over his whole face. Just as he was about to put his arms around me I squirmed and freed myself from his embrace. A big smile came over his face like this was some wonderful game. He tottered to his feet and headed my way. I circled around the huge mahogany desk that dominated the end of the room. It must have been quite a sight—this ancient, stooped old man chasing me around his beautiful desk like [I was] a young secretary."

Just when Drew was about to give in and let Cukor have his way with him, the old man grabbed his back and staggered to an overstuffed chair. He cried out dramatically, demanding that Drew bring him a painkiller from the drawer in his desk. "He was putting on quite a performance. Not to be outdone, I acted horrified and dashed for the medication. We were both quite intense." After he had given Cukor the pill, he helped him upstairs and put him into his bed. A bit later Cukor pushed another button, and the doors were unlocked. "I thanked him for a wonderful evening, and he thanked me for making an old man happy. It was the beginning of a long and cherished friendship."

CHAPTER TEN

The Early Films

Rip Colt, pleased with the reception his not-quite-up-to-standards new star was receiving, kept Drew busy with still-photography sessions and film shoots. His pictures appeared in magazines nationwide, and the Al Parker legend gained strength in the increasingly visible gay subculture. Post-Stonewall gays had been casting about for a new image to fashion themselves after, and Drew-as-Al provided it. Lean, fit, bearded, sexually assured Al Parker embodied the look, the attitude, the substance of what it meant to be a gay man in the '70s and '80s.

Drew's next work for Colt was on a pair of loops, collectively titled *Timberwolves.* Drew is paired with Mike Davis, another in Colt's stable of studly beefcake. Davis, whose real name was Winn Strickland, was a successful set designer who often worked at Las Vegas casinos. Winn, who over the years became Drew's best friend, worked as an occasional costar and frequent set designer for Surge Studio, the film production company

Drew and Richard formed when they decided to cash in on Al's fame and claim a stake in the burgeoning gay-film industry.

As the first loop opens, Al is alone at a rustic cabin in the mountains, wearing some mad '70s designer's take on overalls—skintight with elephant-bell legs. Never fear, however—the Parker physique and prick overcome all obstacles.

Al is eating strawberries like they are cocks when Mike Davis rides up on horseback. Al serves Davis a cup of coffee, and they chat while Al rubs his crotch. Moments later the pair start going at it like rabbits. Both men are very macho, and the sex is direct and to the point. After thoroughly feeling each other up, Davis pulls a bedroll from his saddle and rolls it out on the picnic table. The pair suck each other, then jerk off until Davis comes.

In the second loop Al and Mike are making out by a waterfall. They strip naked and go at it. In a departure for a short loop like this, there is a slow, sexy buildup—the pair kissing and feeling each other up before moving to the main event. Colt pulls back from his performers, putting the men and the sex into the context of the setting's natural beauty. Soon, however, art takes a backseat to a session of rimming that has Al taking tongue up the ass and loving it.

In a rare moment, Al bottoms for Davis on a flat rock in the middle of a mountain stream. The smile is wiped off his face by this turn of events, but he takes it like a man. Then, in a bow to spontaneous reality that Colt probably decided to include in the finished loop because it looked so damned sexy, Davis is seen washing his dick in the stream.

A moment later, back on the rock with Al, Davis prepares to bottom. There is no scowling in this segment. Al is riding hard; Davis, his stiff prick rubbing against Al's belly, has a big smile on his face. Al is an awesome lover, alternately kissing Davis and sucking his cock as he fucks him to climax. When Al is ready for his money shot, he straddles Davis's chest and jerks off into his mouth. The film cuts back to the cabin, where Al and Davis are lip-locked yet again. Before the loop becomes too syrupy, Davis ambles off on his horse, leaving Al alone with his strawberries.

One of the chief delights of this, and of many other of the early eight-millimeter loops, is the spontaneity of the sexual coupling. The direction is minimal, and the sex, when it is inspired, is genuinely erotic. As explained by award-winning gay-film director Jerry Douglas, "It was back at the tail end of the hippie era, when everyone fucked everyone. Unlike today, it was less an industry than it was a lark." This quality shines through in *Timberwolves,* making it a delightfully guilty pleasure.

Hand Tooled, Drew's last film for Colt, was another gem of imaginative filmmaking. In this loop Al is alone in the back of his van with an irrepressible grin on his face. He begins fondling the mounded lump in the crotch of his pants, chattering away into the silence. Throughout the action Al talks to the camera, making the loop a lip reader's delight.

While he is playing with himself, an extra hand reaches around and begins stroking his cock. As the minutes pass more and more hands appear, mauling his now-naked body. Al sucks the fingers on one disembodied hand while another begins fingering his ass. Through it all he is jerking off and continuing his monologue—to the hands? To the camera? To you? Finally, overwhelmed, he shoots a load right over his head and collapses, alone in the van with only the requisite number of hands. Al closes the van door, leaving us with nothing but an enigmatic smile.

Here Al is "The Clone." He has the look—clipped beard; short hair; lean, taut body—and the attitude. He also has all the right moves and a certain indefinable star quality that caused his image to stick in the minds and libidos of thousands of gay men across the country.

For Robert Richards, it was Al's skin. "I'm convinced Drew's stardom was attributable, at least in part, to his skin. I've talked to cameramen and others in the know, and they attribute much of his success to the way he photographed. There is an inner glow when you see him on-screen. It is a very rare quality." There are many times in his films when Al Parker is with someone younger, more muscular, hung bigger, but none of that matters. When he is on-screen, it is almost impossible not to watch him.

Other gay-film makers caught on to Drew's allure, and Al Parker quickly became a hot commodity. Falcon Studios had, like Colt, been in the eight-millimeter loop business since the early '70s. Chuck Holmes, the founder of Falcon Studios, recognized Drew's star potential and offered him work. Drew recognized the opportunity for what it was—additional exposure to the public and a chance to make it with a whole new group of hot guys. He made three loops for Falcon in the mid '70s.

In *Weekend Lock-up* Al runs afoul of the law. After driving a red VW up a winding mountain road Al stops, gets out of the car, pulls down his pants to take a leak, then starts fondling himself through his Jockeys. As soon as Al finishes pissing, a pair of handsome cops come roaring up the road. They cuff him and haul him off to jail. At the jailhouse the officers drag him up the stairs, put him into a cell, and strip him. In contrast to the two brawny cops, Al looks small and boyish.

After roughing him up a bit, they leave him in the cell.

Inexplicably, one of them returns a few moments later with a clean pair of briefs. Al puts them on and lies on the bunk, ready to ignite. The cops come by from time to time to check him out, obviously on the verge of bursting into flames themselves.

When one of the cops starts fondling himself, Al rolls over onto his belly and flashes his ass. The cop goes into the cell, heating up the action. He feels Al up, then begins to devour him, front and rear. Al reciprocates. Then the second cop joins the fray. Both men focus on Al. The hot sex is enhanced by interesting camera angles. Entire bodies, not just body parts, are included in the frame, and much of the action is shot through the cell's bars.

Al tops both cops, employing his soon-to-be-signature jack-hammer style. Again, as in the Colt loops, the action is rough and ready. The participants are obviously enjoying themselves, and nothing seems rehearsed. Al's rose-gold flesh appears illuminated from within, forming a remarkable contrast to the stark white of the cell walls. When the crucial moment arrives, Al is the last man to fire his rockets. In contrast to his costars, he erupts like a geyser, further defining his superstar status. At the fade-out, he grins down at the cop he's straddling while smacking the guy's hairy chest with his glistening erection.

His next outing for Falcon, *Rocks and Hard Places,* is shot in the great outdoors. A cock ring is dropped in the woods. Jeff Turk hears it fall and comes to investigate. Al, in a plaid shirt but missing his pants, is seen in a clearing, looking available. The pair wastes no time in getting together.

After taking a few moments to truss up his privates with a leather shoelace until his cock turns purple—another signature Parker move—the pair proceed to suck each other beside a stream. In an apparent move to add variety, the pair suddenly stumble across a naked man sleeping facedown on a blue tarp in the woods. The dynamic duo kneel and penetrate the man fore and aft; however, all of their attention is focused on each other—the third man is merely there to provide orifices. He is never acknowledged by either Parker or Turk, and he doesn't come.

In *Taxi,* the final loop Drew did for Falcon, he is paired with Craig Graham. The action takes place in a taxi on Southern California's Pacific Coast Highway. Al, the taxi driver, pulls off to the side of the road, where he and his passenger proceed to have sex—outside of the car, right on the highway.

The loop is memorable for costar Graham's ability to shove his cock up his own ass. Al helps enthusiastically, adding a few fingers to the fray. Then he fucks Graham while Graham's own dick is still in his asshole. Al delivers the goods with his veiny wonder of a prick. He mounts the guy and fucks him silly after draping him over the open door of the cab. Afterward, he takes his passenger to the Hyatt Regency and lets him out.

While Drew was having a ball—literally and figuratively—with his new career, his partner Richard was so fed up with his lucrative but boring position as a mid-level executive with an aerospace company that he resigned. A few months previously, the couple had purchased the Hermosa Beach house that Richard had been renting when they met, so they suddenly had financial responsibilities to meet. The film loops Drew had been starring in, although sexually stimulating and ego-boosting, were hardly paying the bills. The guys were left looking for a way to support themselves.

Drew's money at this time was coming primarily from his wallpaper-removal business. This surprisingly lucrative undertaking kept Drew, and later Richard, busy catering to the redecorating whims of Los Angeles matrons. It also provided the financial backing that ultimately made Surge Studio a reality.

Drew had been modeling and performing for Colt and Falcon for over a year but had very little, financially speaking, to show for it. He got the recognition, had sex with a number of the models he had jerked off over as a youth, and made contact with a few celebrity johns, but he hadn't made any real money. His pictures were selling like hotcakes and showing up in virtually every gay magazine that hit the newsstands, but it was Rip Colt who was raking in the cash. Drew was too savvy to let that little detail pass without notice. His work in porn may have begun as a lark, but he realized it could develop into serious money.

One of the things that had stuck with him since his days at the Playboy mansion was the way in which Hugh Hefner had managed to parlay pictures of naked women into a publishing empire. "One day I walked into Hef's library, where he had an issue of each *Playboy* magazine that had ever been published, and I saw that his entire empire had been built on what took up about three feet of shelf space." The seed, planted then, took root and began to grow.

Being an honest man, Drew first took his idea to Rip Colt. He told him that he wanted a cut of the action. "Look," Drew said, "I'll work for you exclusively from now until the end of time if you will give me 1% of the profit that you are making on me. And the man laughed at me." It was the end of their association.

The severing of the Colt connection was no great loss. Drew had gained notoriety as a Colt model and had made enough of a name for himself that he was able to work when and where he pleased. In 1977 he teamed up with the video branch of *The*

Advocate to make *Heavy Equipment.* The project was shot in 3-D and featured, in addition to Al Parker, porn superstars Jack Wrangler, Roger, and the Christie twins. It was an excellent cast, but the sex was secondary to the technology. Over the years the color has washed to shades of blue and gray, and the 3-D effects have ceased to work. The film today is nothing more than a well-intentioned curiosity.

Not so with Drew's next film project. After years of producing their wildly successful loops, Falcon Studios was ready to branch out into feature films. Other studios and directors had been turning out features for a number of years, but Falcon was on the verge of creating a gay-porn masterpiece that would catapult the studio to the forefront of X-rated gay-film making.

Chuck Holmes initiated the long-running FalconPac series—all Falcon features are grouped under the general heading of FALCONPAC and assigned a number as well as a title—with a film titled *The Other Side of Aspen.* Al Parker, Dick Fisk, Jeff Turk, Chad Benson, and Casey Donovan, the man who had made gay-porn history by starring in Wakefield Poole's 1971 classic *Boys in the Sand,* were chosen to costar. The sexual chemistry clicked, and the results were electrifying. The wispy plot revolves around the off-slope shenanigans at an Aspen ski lodge. The performers couple in pairs and groups, setting a high erotic standard for the whole FalconPac series. In their scene together Casey Donovan and Al light up the screen—and bring fisting out of the subculture closet and into the gay mainstream.

Drew and Casey knew each other by reputation but hadn't met before the July day the filming took place. Donovan felt the anonymity was an enhancement for sexual performance. "I think it's easier, because you can perform on a strictly chemical level. Al and I never met until the afternoon we flew from San

Francisco to Lake Tahoe. A couple of hours later we did our first scene together, and he wound up fist-fucking me. Quite an experience!"

Drew put his newly won notoriety to the test in as many arenas as possible. The producers of gay erotica weren't the only people interested in Drew's unique talents. The social climate in Southern California in the post-Stonewall years was one of unbridled hedonism. There were those who had opted for political activism and high seriousness, but the hedonists were carrying the day, and Drew was firmly in their camp. Through his connections at Colt and Falcon he was able to gain entrée to all the most exclusive gay gatherings in Los Angeles. He and Richard were drawn to it—heart, soul, and cock.

The pair was seen all over Los Angeles, rubbing elbows and other salient body parts with the gay elite. Keith Alton, a party boy himself, remembers the pair well. "They turned up everywhere I turned up, and I was everywhere in those days. They were handsome, they were articulate, they were available. Whatever the occasion required, they seemed able to strike the right note. Drew was so spectacularly handsome and hung, and Richard was so accommodating, they were indispensable in many circles."

One of these circles was hosted by screenwriter Bronte Woodard. Woodard had recently struck it rich—instead of accepting a lump-sum payment, he opted for a percentage of the gross for penning a screenplay. The resulting film, *Grease*, went on to break box-office records, making Woodard a millionaire almost overnight. To celebrate, Woodard bought a mansion in the Hollywood hills, furnished it in style by helping himself to items from the major studios' prop warehouses, and set himself up as a grand Hollywood host.

Reinventing gay sex: some Surge Studio classics.

Family portraits: (top) Drew and longtime companion Richard Cole; (inset) Drew, Justin Cade, and Doogie the dog; (bottom) Drew's marijuana pipe, "touched by the lips of so many beautiful men."

Top and bottom photos courtesy of Keith Reiter; inset Justin Cade

On the road: (left) Irresistible challenge in Salt Lake City; (inset, top) An innocent abroad—in Venice, Italy; (inset, bottom) Meeting locals at the state fair.

WARNING

IT IS UNLAWFUL TO COMMIT LEWD ACTS IN A PUBIC AREA SECTION 32-2-5 CO

THIS AREA IS PATROLLED BY THE SALT LAKE CITY POLICE DEPARTMENT

The star: (top) At the premiere of *Flashback;* (lower left) Clone poster art; (lower right) Name above the title. (opposite) The perfect clone; (inset) Skye Dawson in the mask scene from *Turned On.*

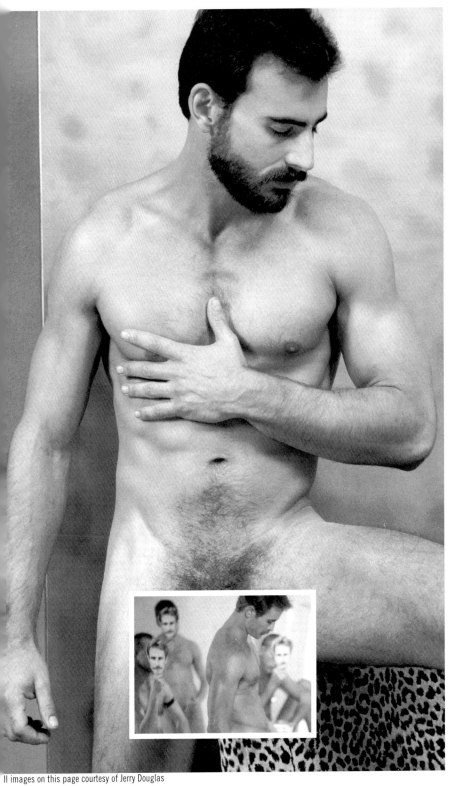

All images on this page courtesy of Jerry Douglas

(left) One of Drew's window constructions; (top right) Doogie, Drew's beloved dog; (bottom right) Drew with his father and a lady friend.

(top) Richard Cole in front of the Hermosa Beach house where he and Drew lived for 16 years; (bottom left) Drew and Keith Reiter's San Francisco home; (bottom right) The interior of Drew's van, a sex pad on wheels.

Top photo courtesy of Justin Cade; others Keith Reiter

(top) Drew an⟨
friends at his
40th birthday;
(center left)
Drew with lon⟨
hair, what Rob⟨
Richards calle⟨
his "Jesus
phase"; (center
right) Drew an⟨
Doogie; (bot-
tom) Drew pos⟨
ing in front of
the San
Francisco sky-
line.

Cousin Janie had recently gotten back into contact with Drew, and she remembers Woodard's house vividly. "Drew had come to my place in New York one day and told me his whole story. It was funny, but he didn't want me to see his movies. I think he felt a little self-conscious about it, maybe because we'd known each other for so long. It didn't mean a damned thing to me one way or another. He was still Drew to me.

"Anyhow, I came out to Los Angeles and stayed with Drew and Richard. We used to go hang out at Bronte's incredible house on Mulholland Drive, which overlooked what seemed to be all of Los Angeles. Bronte was gone much of the time, and Drew and Richard had the run of the place. I never saw any of the wild parties, but I knew they took place."

Within certain circles Woodard gained renown for his orgiastic parties—stocked with the most delectable, most available men in the country. Drew and Richard became party regulars and, eventually, Woodard's close friends. Woodard had surrounded himself with a group of young men from the film industry, many of whom had worked in various capacities on the film version of *Grease*. As the notoriety of these gatherings spread, more and more people clamored for invitations.

Alton was there, watching and remembering. "Drew and Richard were great-looking guys, but then, so was everybody else. I talked to them, and they were quite nice. Drew wasn't going around introducing himself as Al Parker, but if anyone came up to him and asked, 'Say, aren't you...?' he wasn't insulted by the recognition.

"When the guests got down and dirty, Drew and Richard were always in the thick of things. The group sex was very democratic back then. Everybody was getting down with everybody else, not standing around waiting to be admired. Drew's cock was an obvious standout, and he liked the attention it brought him, but he would get as excited as the next guy if another really big cock was on display. It was clear to me that he was fascinated by dicks. The man could suck cock for hours on end."

Drew wasn't by any means the only man in the Los Angeles area with a fixation on size. Many who had this interest also had the money to indulge their whims. For gay men in the film industry especially, discretion was a necessity. Often the easiest way to ensure privacy was to buy a hustler. To be assured of getting the best quality for the money, what better than a preview? The loops produced by the burgeoning male-pornography industry were some of the best audition tapes around.

By his own admission, Drew hustled. However, in later years, he was reticent about discussing this part of his life with friends. Jerry Douglas suspected he only did it when he was desperate for money. Robert Richards felt that he did it because it was expected.

It is clear from the autobiographical notes he left behind that Drew found hustling less than glamorous and far from sexy. Nonetheless, it was an easy way to make good money, and money was often in short supply in the early years before Surge became a moneymaking concern. In addition, the hustling put Drew in contact with people in the industry he wanted to be a part of. Unfortunately, he soon discovered, as had many before him, that an introduction of this kind spelled death to a legitimate career. "I went to film school after I quit medical school but, as is the case with most people, I had trouble finding work. On the big projects, union rules limit you to a small area of the production process. I gradually came to the realization that working on smaller projects was better." In this case, "smaller" meant "X-rated." "You learn all about the movie business that way. You get to do everything—a bit of writing, a little directing, some work with lighting and camera angles. Your ideas and input are valued."

The downside was that his ideas and input were only valued by a very specialized industry. "I discovered that my nude work with Colt pretty much ended any chance of a legitimate career. There was no crossing over. It just wasn't done." He tried doggedly to make it happen. "I worked it. I met everyone there was to meet in Hollywood. They knew who I was and what I'd done, and I knew what they were and what they were after. Still, once you've done porn, they don't ever get past your dick. They think, *Look at this kid. He's hot, he's out there, he's got a big cock. He must be stupid!*"

While Drew struggled to break into mainstream filmmaking, his fame as a sexual icon grew. *The Other Side of Aspen* cemented his star status and brought him to the attention of a man who would enhance his sexual-superstar status and help him to found Surge Studio. This man would become a friend, a business partner, and, ultimately, Drew's most bitter enemy.

CHAPTER ELEVEN

The Steve Scott Films

Salvatore "Sal" Grasso began directing gay X-rated films in 1969, using the name Steve Scott. Grasso had moved to Hollywood after a stint in the Army. While making a name for himself as a director of gay films, he also worked in several capacities on general-market films like *Sextette,* Mae West's last film, based on her play of the same name, and the Ray Milland horror vehicle *Frogs.* Generally speaking, he had better luck with his X-rated career.

In addition to several early loops, Grasso is credited as director on 27 full-length films. Three of these are straight, the rest gay. Scott was a painstaking professional who worked to get the most from his actors and his material. In addition to the loosely strung-together sex scenes which were the stock-in-trade of Falcon, Colt, and Brentwood, Grasso also made what he referred to as "story films," dealing with emotions as well as sex. During their four-year association, Drew had an opportunity to star in and produce both types of Steve Scott films.

By the time Sal met him in 1979, Drew was ready for a major change. Frustrated by the meager financial returns offered by an acting career in porn and thwarted in his efforts to break into the Hollywood mainstream, Drew had been toying with the idea of starting his own studio. This idea had been germinating since Rip Colt laughed him out of his office. "I had the background in film, so I decided to try and do it myself," he told Jerry Douglas. "Richard and I started to take stills because we didn't have the expertise or the money to do a film. Before I get involved in anything I like to test the waters. I wasn't familiar with mail order for the photos, and I didn't know much about producing a porn film. So we did things in very small steps."

Enter Steve Scott. He met Drew at a party that *In Touch* magazine threw to celebrate Al Parker's debut as its most recent cover model and centerfold. "Sal later told me that he walked into the party, saw me from across the room, and asked who I was. The guy he'd asked said in this hushed voice, 'That's Al Parker,' like I was really something. Anyway, Sal approached me about doing a full-length feature film. Not a loop, but a feature. He'd done half a dozen films by this time and was an established name in the business. Naturally, I was very interested to see how a feature film was made." An agreement was struck. Drew and Richard were slated to star as lovers in Grasso's newest picture.

Inches was produced by TMX for the now-defunct 55th Street Playhouse in New York City. This was the theater that, at the beginning of the decade, had screened the premiere of *Boys in the Sand,* a landmark production that ushered in a new era of gay-film making. Drew called *Inches* "the first upper-middle-class sex movie. It was more than just a sex movie. The people in it had jobs and clothes and places to live. The characters had a life beyond the sex, which made it interesting."

In the film Al Parker gets top billing—justifiably so, because he looks every bit the fantasy of a porn star. His body is perfectly sculpted, his bearded face movie-star handsome, his long eyelashes impossibly thick. The lighting makes him appear luminous; it is a dazzling effect. Even Drew fell under Al's spell: "I thought I looked good in *Inches*. The lighting was very carefully worked out. It was the first time I ever spoke on film."

In the first scene Al is in bed with Richard, trying to tell him about a disturbing dream he has had, in which Richard has been unfaithful. Richard shrugs it off and goes to shower. After a dual JO scene—Al in the bed, awash in apricot light; Richard in the shower—the pair separate, the growing rift in their relationship painfully obvious.

The scene changes to the photo studio and gallery where Al works. A photographer whose work is being exhibited tries to seduce him, but Al refuses. There is real acting here. It is quite clear that Drew can carry his weight in a dramatic scene.

That night, after a very unsatisfactory encounter, Richard informs Al that they are through. He has met someone new while on a business trip to San Francisco and is in love. A fantasy scene ensues, wherein Richard displays his oral prowess with an impressive lineup of cocks. The close-ups of Al as he watches in dismay are a sight to behold.

The balance of the film focuses on Al and his attempts to enter the freewheeling gay life of the '70s. He picks up a co-worker who's out hitchhiking and lets the man blow him after a feeble protest that he isn't ready to play around so soon after ending his relationship.

Back at the gallery Al quarrels with the photographer who had tried to pick him up earlier in the day. Al then goes to a sex club, where he watches but doesn't participate. He does, however, encounter and then agree to go to the country with the photographer he had snubbed earlier.

After a very sexy nude romp in the snow—real snow, at that—the pair make love in front of a fireplace with sweet, slow music on the sound track. The next day, as they are driving back to the city, Al rethinks his priorities and decides he has some catching up to do.

Drew played completely against type here, portraying a monogamous kind of guy who genuinely disliked the idea of people who just sucked cock and counted tricks. The hedonistic thrust of the film was what he and the pre-AIDS era were all about. In many ways, *Inches* was a how-to manual for clones. The primary relationship was broken up, and sex between strangers was lauded as the ideal. The film's final scene was couched in romantic terms—soft music and firelight—but portrayed recreational sex without commitment.

Inches established Drew as a force to be reckoned with in the industry. "That's when I began to realize there was a market for Al Parker, whereas I wasn't sure before because I was just a skinny kid from a Boston suburb." His newfound fame had its price, driving a stake through the heart of any hopes he may have still harbored of working in the mainstream market.

Before *Inches* was released, Drew had convinced Allan Carr, producer of the megahit *Grease,* to give him a chance. He had first seen Carr years earlier when he was working at the Playboy mansion, but really got to know him through their mutual friend, Bronte Woodard. Drew was hired as assistant director for Carr's production of *Can't Stop the Music,* a delightfully cheesy disco-beat musical romp starring the Village People, Bruce Jenner, Steve Guttenberg, and Valerie Perrine. According to one review, the movie featured "terrible lines, awful acting, ridiculous musical numbers, and a totally inane plot." Still, it was a Hollywood movie, and it offered a foot in the door of legitimate filmmaking.

Unfortunately for Drew, *Inches* opened the very day he started his new job on location in New York City. "My face was on posters all over Greenwich Village. Nobody I was working with knew what I was doing with my 'other' career. When Carr found out he went ballistic. He thought it was very bad publicity and that people would now think he was making a gay picture." After watching the Village People belt out "YMCA" in a hunk-filled locker room, there is little doubt that Carr was right to worry. In any case, it was bad timing on Drew's part.

Carr wouldn't let go of the issue, forcing Drew's hand. "I didn't want any trouble with him. The man was acting like a jerk, so I quit the project. I ultimately had the satisfaction of knowing that my little film played in theaters for a year, and his sank out of sight in less than a month."

This was the last time Drew sought help for his career. "I figured that from then on, I had to go it on my own. It was obvious that nobody was going to give me anything. I figured that if I couldn't do it on my own, something must be wrong with me. I determined that I was going to start my own company and make my own films." He decided that he was also going to be in charge of marketing, which meant utilizing mail order. He knew that mail order could be very lucrative, even though his one previous venture, Worm World, had failed—due to neglect more than anything else. Now, however, he had Richard and was confident that together they would make it work.

He had been unable to get distribution rights to the still photographs when he starred in *Inches* but did not make the same mistake when he and Scott made their next feature together, once again with TMX producing. "When we made

Wanted I made the agreement with TMX that I would do the stills and have all distribution rights to them." This was something of a coup. Since there was a very limited market for celluloid, the production stills were almost as valuable as the film. There was also a new technology on the horizon that Drew suspected had a great potential. "I knew full well that these movies had limited possibilities for a theatrical run. I figured that video was the wave of the future, and I wanted the rights to sell the videos."

Although shot in only two days, *Wanted* proved to be another first-rate production with a powerhouse cast. Jack Wrangler plays an abusive warden; Al Parker and Will Seagers are featured as prisoners who escape from a chain gang, still chained together. Seagers's character is straight, and the tension rises as he tries to understand Parker's sexual preferences. Al tells of being raped in a prison shower by two inmates, a tale captured in vivid flashbacks.

There is another very hot flashback scene with Al and Richard together. Drew filled Robert Richards in on the gory details during a taped interview: "It's our latest gimmick—as you know, you gotta have a gimmick. My new stunt in *Wanted* is cramming my balls and my dick up Richard's ass and fucking him." (Richard can be heard in the background complaining, "All that goes up my ass, and he gets star billing!") "You've got to stun and amaze the masses, you know. It came out rather well on film, I think. It pops out like an afterbirth."

In the final scene Al gives Seagers a blow job. Seagers responds in the way a straight male would—he is restrained and nervous but obviously enjoys the experience. The photography, the high quality of the acting, and the harmonica and guitar music on the sound track combine to make *Wanted* memorable. With one exception near the end of his life, this was the last film Drew would make for any company other than his own.

Drew and Richard began searching for a name for their new company. As often seemed to be the case throughout Drew's life, the name came to him purely by accident. "When I was doing *Taxi Driver* for Falcon, we were on location at a farm. I was poking around in the barn and found an old metal sign advertising a milking company called Surge. The sign said SURGE—FASTER MILKING, CLEANER MILK." Drew saw the salacious humor inherent in the sign and took it. "I used to like to take a little souvenir of each movie I did. This one ended up on my bathroom wall over the toilet."

The inspiration came only after much fruitless searching. "For the longest time Richard and I were racking our brains for a good name for our new company. I wanted a name that implied motion, action. Then one afternoon I was taking a leak and staring at that old sign. I remember thinking, *Surge...now, there's a great name.* I subsequently found out that Surge is a tough word for people to pronounce—it doesn't exactly roll off the tongue. Still, it was the word I had been looking for."

Drew and Richard were in New York City promoting *Wanted* when they first met Robert Richards. "I met Drew New Year's Eve, 1979," Richards recalled. "It was in a hotel on Times Square. And," he added, with undisguised smugness, "I didn't get back home until long after the New Year's revelers had given up the ghost."

Drew arrived for the interview with Richard, which gave Rob Richards quite a start. "Richard Cole was the first grown man I had ever seen naked. I was a youngster on a tour of the school I would attend the next year. They took us into the boys' locker room, and there he was, walking toward us, naked. He must have been a senior, because he was very definitely a man with a hairy chest. It was an image that I carried with me to adulthood."

After some prompting Cole vaguely remembered the incident. He was amused by Richards's tale, and the men bonded instantly. Richards was also pleased to discover that Al Parker's alter ego, Drew Okun, was a man of substance. "I think we all realized that we were real people who had this strange attraction to something that was just beginning to become socially acceptable. Porn was a part of the sexual liberation that had been sweeping the gay community since the early '70s." Drawing on this rapport, Richards got the young entrepreneur to speak freely.

"It really has been fun," Drew admitted when asked about his trip to New York. "The thing is, I'm busy and I don't have time for personal appearances. Starring in porn films definitely doesn't pay the bills. It pays so little, as a matter of fact, that I was looking to get something else out of it and asked for two plane tickets to New York. Our director, Steve Scott, came through for us. That's the only reason we were able to come.

"Being a porn star, people come to see me expecting me to do a live sex show. I've been telling them I feel it is more personal to talk to them rather than just be on the stage jerking off. I want involvement with the audience. I want to talk to them and find out what they want in a good porn film. If they want to see my dick, they can watch the movie. It looks better on film, anyway."

Richards found this quirk quite telling. "Drew was always afraid people would be disappointed in him in person. He had begun his career in the days of movies and was used to seeing himself blown up big. He loathed personal appearances, and there was never any sexual performing on a stage. He seemed to feel that real life diminished him."

Drew noted this disjunction between life and fantasy in an interview he did years later for *Advocate Men*. "It would be much better for me to slip into Al Parker 24 hours a day. Unfortunately, he is only brought out of the closet a couple of times a year. The rest of the time, I'm just Drew."

While in New York City, Drew took the still photos from *Wanted* around to the gay-magazine publishers, meeting Jerry Douglas in the offices of *Stallion* along the way. Encouraged by the reception he got, he and Richard followed up with several other photographic scenarios for magazines. "We had a million ideas—scenarios like 'Pit Stop,' 'The Stretch,' 'Surf's Up,' and we were doing everything you had to do for a film except have a motion-picture camera crew. We'd put out the magazines for the mail-order market, and we'd get all these people writing to ask, 'Is there an eight-millimeter loop version available?' And we'd have to write back and say, No, there wasn't. That's what made us think we should go from still production to film."

Even with rights to the stills, they weren't making any headway. "With the magazines, we had to work through distributors, and they were making all the money." Surge was putting out six magazines and barely breaking even. Drew and Richard realized that they had to be completely independent to get ahead.

The response to *Inches* and *Wanted* had also reaffirmed their conviction that Al Parker was a very marketable commodity. Drew told Robert Richards, "I'm amazed that my career in porn has lasted as long as it has. I mean, I'm more surprised than anyone that anybody cares about me on film. I've been breaking box-office records here in New York when I make a personal appearance at the theater. I'm popular now because nobody new and super hot has come along lately. One magazine a few years back said that I was part of the 'spring collection' for 1976, along with Roger and Mike Davis. Maybe it's my eyes. I've always heard stars capture the audience with their eyes. That's how Bette Davis did it, anyway."

As Surge got off the ground, Drew and Richard were fortunate that a niche was opening up that they could fill. Falcon was giving up its magazine trade to concentrate on the films. Rip Colt was backing away from the free-for-all hard-core films that had established his reputation as one of the pioneering figures in male erotica. He was turning his attention to solo JO loops and soft-core photography of the body beautiful. "I think they're all worried about getting into trouble with the FBI," Drew mused to Richards on the eve of the '80s. "Throughout the '70s there's been trouble with censorship of pornography. The established companies are backing off because they've made it already. As for me, I've got nothing to lose if they come after me. You can't get blood out of a turnip, as they say. We're doing hard-core magazines right now— nobody else is. I know we'll get flack from the government about it, but it's what I want to do. Right now I'm being very careful about my taxes. I figure they'll get me for taxes, not the porn. Besides, I'll only keep doing this as long as it's fun and profitable. I'm still hoping for something to happen with legitimate films. If you'd told me back when I was a premed student in Boston that everybody would be calling me 'Al' and that I'd be making my living doing mail-order porn, I would've said you were crazy."

CHAPTER TWELVE

The Birth of Surge Studio

The personal appearances in New York had been a blast. Drew and Richard had been galvanized by the reception they received and knew the time was ripe to capitalize on their current fame. Money, however, was still in critically short supply. Cash soon came their way, but there were significant strings attached.

"I met somebody who *said* he was a film producer. He talked a good line and suggested that we should do a film together. Richard and I talked it over and, against our better judgment, we said yes. Then the guy told me that he wanted Kip Noll to be in the film. He told me he knew Kip personally. 'I can get him,' he assured me. The man was going to put up all the money, and I was going to direct, produce, and star in the film. I should've known it was too good to be true."

Despite their misgivings they got the cast and crew together and shot *Flashback,* Surge Studio's first film, with Drew at the helm as director, producer, and featured performer. Richard was deeply involved in all aspects of production, but he was content to remain in the background and let Drew take the credit. *Flashback* was shot on a shoestring budget, but it does have one prop worthy of mention. A rattan chair figures in the first scene of the movie—and it was a very special chair indeed.

Bronte Woodard had died suddenly in August 1980 of liver failure complicated by acute hepatitis. When Drew and Richard got the news, they rushed over to Bronte's mansion before the executors of Woodard's estate were able to secure it and let themselves in. Since they were such good friends, they expected to be legatees. They searched Bronte's papers, looking for a copy of his will. They weren't in it. Undaunted, the pair went through the house, commandeering artwork and furnishings. Among the items of furniture they acquired was the rattan garden set used in George Cukor's film *The Women,* starring Joan Crawford, Norma Shearer, Rosalind Russell, and a host of other female luminaries of '30s Hollywood. The next time you see this classic, pay special attention to the scenes at Marjorie Main's Reno divorce ranch. Joan Fontaine sits in this very chair out in the yard while pouring out her sorrows to Norma Shearer.

The plot of *Flashback* is paper-thin. Al is being photographed by Kurt Mannheim with a view to creating a portfolio of nude studies. As the sex gets under way, Al is seated in the famous rattan chair, masturbating. Watching him, it becomes clear that the man had a fixation on his own genitals. He stares at his cock as though mesmerized by it. "Drew was always focused on his dick," Robert Richards mused. "His self-esteem depended not so much on his looks as on his cock. It was really what he was about."

As the scene proceeds, Al reaches orgasm, then in a fantasy follow-up, Mannheim sets his camera aside and joins the action. As the pair couples in the chair, the camera glides around, taking in the action in both close-up and full body shots. Drew as director—with the uncredited help of Sal Grasso—proved adept at photographing the sex act. He focused on the salient detail yet never lost sight of the importance of the face and body as gauges of sexual response.

Drew, always a master of self-promotion, never missed a chance to plug his new studio and his own earlier films. In one scene he makes a phone call and identifies his company as Surge Studio while standing in front of framed posters for *Inches* and *Wanted*.

Kip Noll, the man Al is calling, was the one and only reason the film received funding. He was the hot young thing the money man was hoping to seduce, so he was the one Drew was saddled with as a costar. It was not a happy pairing. "I was not impressed with Kip Noll," Drew told Jerry Douglas in an interview years after the fact. "I never saw him as the boy next door. He was unkempt, ungroomed, arrogant, a street person. But he was a star, for whatever reason. I was looking for a Colt type, a Falcon type, not a street type. Unfortunately, I wasn't in a position where I could say, 'Get your hair cut or else.' Still, I was glad enough to have him in my movie."

Noll first appears in a scene with another slender, blond street type. The two tangle in front of a huge Wurlitzer jukebox. Although well-photographed, with plenty of graphic detail, the scene is somewhat of a letdown after Al's dynamic performance with Mannheim. Al Parker was always a very hard act to follow.

The next scene, with Scott Taylor, was Drew's favorite in the film. Taylor appeared in a number of Surge films over the years, almost always performing solo. "I think he is one of the most erotic people in this business, even though he only has sex with himself. He's amazing. I mean, you just can't pay somebody to be as crazy as Scott Taylor is in a movie." They had been slated to appear in a scene together in a Steve Scott film titled *R.J. and the Kid.* Unfortunately, that project fell victim to a wrecked rental car, and their coupling never took place. By the time of *Flashback* Taylor was only willing to blow himself, so Drew agreed to let him appear on his own terms. "So he did the autofellatio scene, and I think it is the hottest scene in the movie."

Al appears here only in the guise of the photographer who captures the scene on film. Always a connoisseur of the offbeat, Drew as director works to capture Taylor's technique from every angle. The scene does amaze—Taylor licks, sucks, and deep-throats himself, even managing to lick his own balls. There are a number of excellent close-ups of this very intimate communion, until Taylor pops off in his own mouth.

As was often the case in the early Surge films, Richard makes an appearance, this time playing the role of a man interested in buying Al's photographs. The pair have another cinematic go at Al Parker's ball-inserting specialty. More than any other porn performer before or since, Al Parker made his balls a distinct part of the sexual experience, not just window dressing that dangled in the background. He manipulates his gonads like they were made of brass, cramming them up Richard's ass like a butt plug. There they remain for most of the scene, keeping the pair joined while Al alternately brandishes his cock and shoves it up Richard's ass.

In the final scene Al and Kip have their fated meeting. The scene is set at Drew and Richard's Hermosa Beach house, which would see action in many guises over the years as Surge Studio's main soundstage. The big question, up until the moment the camera began to roll, was: What the hell were they going to do with each other?

Aside from Drew's distinct lack of interest, there was the matter of how they might go about having sex. "It was like a Mexican standoff," he confided to Douglas. "I am not a bottom, and Kip is not a bottom, and I was not gonna let him screw me. I am not fond of being fucked. It has nothing to do with a head trip, because I've done it many times on film. I may look like I'm enjoying it, but I don't find it comfortable. Anyway, I didn't want to get fucked, and I knew Kip didn't want to get fucked, and I also knew there were gonna be tomatoes on the screen if the two of us didn't do something together. The mutual masturbation sequence seemed the most diplomatic way to have that happen." The result, although impressive from the standpoint of sheer penis volume, fails to sizzle. They sprawl side by side, barely touching, not looking at one another, watching masturbation loops while pumping their own towering erections to orgasm. The photography is excellent, the close-ups are impressive, and the money shots are competently captured, but there is no chemistry between the two, and the scene is totally flat.

Overall, *Flashback* showed a great deal of promise for Drew as director and proved that Surge Studio could produce a quality product. Unfortunately, Drew and the producer had been at odds with one another since the project began. "Right away it became very clear that this guy had no idea how to make an X-rated film. All he was thinking was that this was a way of getting into Kip Noll's pants, and that's all he was interested in."

Drew felt cornered, but he was determined to succeed with his dream of becoming a filmmaker, so he persevered. He hadn't been slated to direct but felt that he had no choice. "I was too embarrassed to call Sal Grasso and scream for help." He did finally call Sal to ask for advice, which was willingly given. "I learned a lot from Sal. His forte was making one dollar look like five. He was very kind to me, and he probably told me more about this business than he told anybody else. I was very lucky in that I always worked with good people in the industry. I always tried to hire the best as well."

Once the film was in the can, more problems arose. "Immediately after the film was finished, I was called by somebody named J. Brian. This man told me that he was making a film called *Flashbacks* and that I should change the title of my film." Drew, green and brash, didn't have a clue that J. Brian was a pioneer in the field of gay-male erotica, having produced and directed many of the first gay hits. Brian is primarily remembered today for the erotic classic *Seven in a Barn.*

Drew told Brian that his film was done and that Brian should change the title of *his* movie. "I really didn't know who the man was. I told him that I'd call mine *Al Parker's Flashback,* and he could call his *J. Brian's Flashback,* and we'd just see what happened." Brian chose not to provoke a showdown over the title. *J. Brian's Flashback* was Brian's last film.

In addition, more problems arose between Drew and the producer. After much agonizing discussion and juggling of finances, Drew and Richard bought the man out. The film was theirs. It took virtually every penny they had to purchase the film and all the rights, so the movie had to be a success, or they'd be bankrupt. "My back was up against the wall. Perhaps your best strokes of genius come at times like that. I couldn't afford to fail—I had to save the farm."

He had lots of footage, and he had a vision. "I had an idea of what I wanted to do. I knew what to ask of myself. I know what's hot and what's not hot. No one has to tell me what angle is hot. I know where the camera should be at any given time." Armed with this certainty, Drew and Richard rented an editing room and went into postproduction.

Flashback had been shot over the course of three weekends, and there was enough footage for two movies. Once he got rid of the original producer, he put his own spin on it, shooting new scenes and taking it in another direction entirely. Then he made a wise decision—he swallowed his pride and called his pal Sal. "I said, 'Look, I've shot this film, and now I need help in putting it together.' " They spent the next six weeks in postproduction. "It was at this time that I learned you could make anything happen in a movie. By positioning the pieces of film you can make things happen that never happened in real life. And that's the magic of movies."

Flashback was released in New York at the 55th Street Playhouse. Drew attended the premiere and was reassured. "I knew it was a success. In those days one run at a theater like that could pay for the production. And there were other theaters popping up all over the country. You could make a nice little profit."

Drew left that profit, and all the business details, in Richard's capable hands. Richard was the financial brain behind Surge Studio, the man whose steady hand at the helm made it a thriving enterprise. As with all business, however, some lessons are learned the hard way. After *Flashback* was released Surge was approached by Le Salon with an offer to purchase the video rights. Inexplicably, given Drew's musings on the future of video when he was making *Inches* and *Wanted*, he agreed to Le Salon's offer. Bottom line: He and Richard were desperate for cash. Characteristically, Drew tried to talk himself into thinking he'd done the right thing. "I thought video was a throwaway, a by-product—you know, sell the video rights for, oh, a couple of hundred bucks. We figured it was gravy. So we sold them the video rights, and they sold maybe 25 tapes when our film was released theatrically. Hardly worth noticing." After the release of the next Surge feature, however, they would most definitely notice it.

Although Drew claimed to believe that video rights to his films were a throwaway, he was fascinated by the technology. So much so, in fact, that he purchased his own video camera in 1981. At that point the apparatus was still cumbersome, but Drew adapted to it and never looked back. Throughout the remaining 11 years of his life, it seemed that he recorded everything—holiday vacations, home remodels, strolls along the beach in front of his home. Nothing was too mundane to capture his interest. He left behind miles of videotape—a record of his life and times. The camera became an extension of his eyes: turning, cruising, watching with him as he went about his daily life.

One of his first efforts as he began to learn the ins and outs of his new toy was a bathroom remodel at the house in Hermosa Beach. Throughout their life together Drew and Richard were always remodeling something. In this instance, it was a major bathroom overhaul, and Drew recorded every stage, from demolition to the first shower. He began as Richard and Winn Strickland were cutting a hole in the roof for a skylight. The tape unfolded much like the buildup for a porn film, focusing on chests, thighs, and crotches. Richard, always at risk when in range of Drew's prying video eye, was later seen naked in the half-finished bath.

Drew also spent countless hours and miles of videotape recording street life in Hermosa Beach. He would often walk the block and a half to the beach with his dog, Doogie, and spend the morning scanning the beach, getting footage of sand and surf on the beach near the pier. Many of these shots were later used as setups in his films.

The camera also provided a great mask to hide behind while cruising the inhabitants of the intensely urban Los Angeles–area beach community that was his neighborhood. He always had an eye out for thighs and crotches, chests and faces. Drew was, as the tapes make abundantly clear, a voyeur. Popular sex icon Al Parker was the pose; the lonely youngster from suburban Massachusetts who spent his days observing the world around him was the reality. He had a director's eye, obsessively observing the space, light, movement, and volume of the jumbled beach scene around him. The sound tracks of these tapes consisted of ambient street noises, overlaid by Drew's stream-of-consciousness monologue about any and every thing that captured his attention, however briefly. It evolved into a diary, kept on spools of tape.

Drew's mania remained unabated, even when in company. On Christmas Day, 1981, Drew and Richard had friends over for drinks and dinner. The camera was still relatively new and Drew's excitement level was high. The technology was novel enough so that the guests all appear to be fascinated by it. Drew, of course, happily explained the wonders of it to anyone willing to peer through the viewfinder. "It looks like Drew is going to have a permanent growth on his shoulder," one friend observed wryly, his comment caught by the microphone.

These tapes not only captured Drew's very personal view of the world, they provide a nostalgic view of the beginning of the '80s. At the party, handsome young men who had perfected the clone look that was sweeping the gay world at the time sat around Drew and Richard's living room, smoking dope while discussing their lives and upcoming projects. And then there was Drew, the host, wandering around his own party, watching it unfold through the camera's lens like a movie on TV. It is all eerily reminiscent of his old employer Hugh Hefner, pajama-clad, sneaking peeks of his parties through balcony railings.

Later, after the guests had departed, Drew's camera followed Richard into the bedroom. It watched him undress and walk into the bathroom, where he filled the new tub, lit candle stubs and set them on the exposed framing in the unfinished room. That done, Richard slipped into the steaming water. Drew's camera eye focused on his lover's handsome, bearded face, caressed his sculpted body, and slowly slid down his torso to his crotch. Drew then panned the room, pausing at the mirror where his own reflection shimmered in the candlelight. The torso, lean and tightly muscled, was unmistakable, as was the famous Al Parker cock, hanging down dark and dangerous between his thighs. But then, in place of Drew's handsome face, there was the camera, on his shoulder, its single red eye winking steadily. It is an arresting image.

CHAPTER THIRTEEN

The Surge Collaborations With Steve Scott

Flashback was making the theatrical circuit, and Surge, although financially shaky, was a going concern. Drew and Richard were also continuing their photo business, marketing their magazines by mail order. They were also still involved with the wallpaper stripping business, which provided the money to keep them afloat. And when times got tough, a discreet ad would appear in the classified pages of *The Advocate*, listing the name Al Parker and a telephone number. There were no explanatory details in the ad. None were necessary. Drew's hustling was a high-end operation. He kept a private phone line and a black book of customers. He was very select—and very expensive. If the prospective client was willing and able to pay the substantial fee, he could view Al Parker in the flesh, up close and as personal as he dared to be.

On the domestic front, Drew's cousin Janie had moved

from New York City to Hermosa Beach. "I had gone through a really bad breakup with a guy in New York," she said, "and Drew told me to come on out and he'd help me find a place to live. He was so wonderful to me. He took me under his wing and helped me get set up. I ended up right next door to him. We hung around together a lot. Drew was like family to me—always there for me, always very important to me. We were neighbors until he moved to San Francisco after Richard's death.

"I was writing a lot of songs at the time, so Drew would hear me working on the same song all day long. He loved to tease me. He'd lean out the window and call my name—'Janie. Oh, Janie.' When I'd answer, he'd scream back in a shrill voice, 'Shut up!' Naturally, I'd respond by playing and singing just a little louder. He'd throw up his hands, shake his head, and go on about his business.

"Drew loved steaks, and we'd often have barbecues out on the beach. Drew would cook for everybody. He loved to get people together and cook for them. He made Thanksgiving feasts every year. He was so good-hearted and down-to-earth. He really cared about other people."

Janie's roommate Phyllis also became a part of Drew and Richard's extended family. "I used to help Rich and Drew with their mail-order business," Phyllis recalled. "I'd package and send out the videos, working there in their house. They were both great guys. Drew would do anything to help his friends. When one friend got pulled over for a DUI, Drew came up with the cash to bail her out of jail. Anytime Janie was in a bind, he'd reach into his pocket and help her out. He was kind, protective, and a really good friend.

"Drew was incredibly creative. One year, he was out painting his house, and he got paint splatters on this pair of Chinese slippers he was wearing. He thought they were cool and wore them around for quite awhile, telling anyone who asked about them that he was going to paint shoes and market them. He didn't, so I took it upon myself to do it instead. I actually made money on the scheme."

Also on hand were Dean and Wolf, two guys who lived across the alley from Drew and Richard and became their intimate friends. "Wolf's bedroom looked into Drew and Richard's living room," Dean recalled. "We talked back and forth across the alley for years. Drew was a great guy. He had a terrific wit about him. He had two distinct personas—Drew and Al Parker. I didn't really know Al Parker because I didn't run with that crowd.

"We all hung out together on the beach. We always went to the Fifth Street lifeguard station. Whenever they were shooting a film at their house Winn Strickland would be there as well, and we'd all hang around and shoot the shit, then they'd go back to the house and go to work."

Dean and Drew often went biking along the strand. "Drew wouldn't wear underwear, so when we went biking, he'd have to change into some longer shorts so he wouldn't expose himself. We'd go out for a ride, taking the same route and cruising the same boys every time." Dean also tried to interest Drew in jogging, but his famous balls got in the way, and the experiment had to be abandoned. "We made it about two blocks, and Drew had to quit. His balls were banging so hard against his legs that he couldn't take it." Considering the abuse those mighty gonads took on film over the years, it's hard to believe he couldn't take the discomfort. Perhaps, Drew just didn't like to run.

From his vantage point across the narrow alley, Dean had ample opportunity to observe the domestic arrangements at the

Hermosa Beach house. "Drew and Richard were perfectly in tune with each other. They had a great domestic life together. They were genuinely together as a couple. To my knowledge, they didn't even maintain separate friendships. They went to a lot of parties, but when they were at home, most of the time it was just the family hanging out together, barbecuing."

Frequently people who weren't a part of the family hung around outside the house. As Al Parker became more and more well-known, groupies swarmed around him, fascinated by the on-screen persona of Al Parker, clone extraordinaire. Some found their way into Drew's bed, some into his films. Others just hung around because it was their nature to worship celebrity.

Janie was often delegated to distract them from their primary target. "Drew had lots of groupies. He was nice to everybody, so they hung around. It seemed like these guys always got foisted off on me, especially the ones who wanted to be friends with him because they thought he really was Al Parker." Janie chuckled slyly. "When these guys ended up at my house—which was right next door, remember—I'd take advantage of their presence. I was always in need of something, and I'd get them to help me out. Unfortunately, then I'd be stuck with them. I never quite understood it, but guys who were fixated on Drew would become fascinated with me because I was so close to him. I was a celebrity by proxy."

Sometimes this celebrity status had its perils. "There was this guy named Teddy. He was a big, overweight, hairy guy who had the hots for Drew. I didn't have a car, and I needed to run some errands, so Teddy offered to drive me around Hollywood. Well, Teddy drove like a lunatic. I had both feet braced on the floor and a death grip on the door's armrest. I kept screaming at him to slow down before we both got killed, and he kept on telling me, 'Hold your tits. Hold your tits.' I told Drew about it, and the guy became Hold Your Tits Teddy for as long as he hung around. He ultimately started getting pretty obnoxious and wouldn't leave us alone. I think it was Richard who finally sent him packing."

Drew and Richard also liked to get out of town—probably to escape the groupies—often driving across the desert to Las Vegas. There, they'd hang out with Winn Strickland while he created elaborate settings for banquets and parties in the casinos. Drew, with his new camera in tow, would follow Winn, recording every detail as he transformed a sterile warehouse-like banquet space into a tropical paradise or a winter cityscape. Drew would trail along after Winn, watching, eavesdropping, cruising through the camera's eye. Afterward there would be parties in private rooms, people sitting shoulder-to-shoulder on the beds, drinking and talking. And there was Drew, standing in a corner, taping and watching as the party swirled around him. Unfortunately for us, but lucky for Drew, when things got really interesting, he'd switch off the camera and join the fray.

When Sal Grasso approached Drew to make a second film, Drew jumped at the chance. "I truly loved working with film," Drew told Jerry Douglas during one of their long interviews for *Manshots* magazine. "Working with Sal was a lot of fun. Besides, it sure as hell was better than scraping wallpaper off of Mrs. Jones's walls.

"I'd always wanted to be a producer of films, not really a director or an actor. For me, acting was strictly a way of becoming a producer. I liked putting it all together: getting the best people to do their best work behind the camera, getting the hottest people I could find and putting them together in front of the camera. I often felt like Mickey Rooney and Judy Garland. You know, 'Let's rent a barn and put on a show.' So I was thrilled by Sal's suggestion. We got together and came up with a movie called *Turned On*. It's probably the most bizarre thing I've ever done, and it's still my favorite film."

Turned On is a celebration of hot, anonymous sex with multiple partners—another version of the gay man's fantasy of liberation in the post-Stonewall, pre-AIDS era. The action opens in a bar, where Al sees handsome, blond Sky Dawson across a crowded bar. Dawson disappears, and Al goes to seek him out. However, Al is distracted from his quest. He opens a toilet stall, sees a guy sitting on the toilet jerking off, and hauls out the Parker prick for a quick servicing. Dawson enters and lets himself be taken just as easily, sucked off by a guy at the trough-style urinal. Throughout the scene Al and Dawson cruise each other, ignoring their respective sex partners.

Al goes home, falls asleep, and dreams of the mysterious blond. His dreams take him to a bathhouse. "I was hanging with a group of people that owned a bathhouse called Mac's. It was a really beautiful facility with a beautiful auditorium space. It was the perfect place to shoot a film."

The extended fantasy sequence in the baths contains some of the most famous footage Al Parker ever appeared in. First, there is the locker scene, with Al opening doors and leaning in to service all the disembodied cocks that are thrust at him. Then there is the scene where Al takes on a roomful of faceless jockstrapped guys on pedestals: "Just me doing the world," he would quip in a later interview. Assisted by Dawson, he chews and sucks them all.

Assembling the cast for these group scenes had been remarkably easy. "We'd put up notices in the bathhouse that we would be shooting a movie, and anyone who wanted to should show up at 10 o'clock in the morning. We wouldn't show their faces and would pay them 25 dollars. And lo and behold, it seemed like the whole world showed up."

The centerpiece of the film was Scott Taylor's solo act on a pedestal. "The person I have to thank the most is Scott Taylor. He had done such a nice job for me in *Flashback,* and I knew he was such an exhibitionist that I asked him how he'd like to do his thing in front of a whole group of people. 'We'll make this crazy set for you,' I told him, 'with neon and a pedestal with a Plexiglas bottom.' Of course, he agreed."

The performance is a tour de force of the bizarre—as always, an Al Parker specialty. It was a performance that almost didn't come off, however. Just as they were ready to shoot Taylor's scene, the lights went out. "For some reason, we blew a fuse. There was no power, and I was sweating bullets. We had a whole crowd gathered, and they were starting to get restless. So we had to go out on a Sunday morning and find 500 feet of extension cord and then plug it into an outlet at the gas station across the street.

"We finally got the power back on, and Scott did his thing. Not only did he suck himself off, he fucked himself—not only did he stick his dick up his ass, but his balls too. It was the show of shows."

After that spectacle there was more to come, including the clone sequence, which serves up every sexual stereotype in the canon, Village People–style. And, of course, the inspired final scene—Sky Dawson in a roomful of men, all holding masks with his likeness imprinted on them. "We had all these people who didn't want their faces shown. We knew the story was going to revolve around me looking for Sky Dawson, which gave me the idea for the masks. I took a black-and-white photo of him, and we had copies made, and we cut them out and stuck them on hat pins so the guys could hold them in front of their faces."

Interspersed throughout the film are vignettes of Al and Dawson coupling—as Al's sex partners of the moment are transformed into the elusive blond by Al's fevered imagination. Dawson is in almost every scene and is at least as important as Al in anchoring the sex.

"Sky Dawson was wonderful. I had seen him in a Falcon film and really wanted to work with him. I approached him, but he was very reluctant to do it for personal reasons. I was relentless, and I finally convinced him to do it. 'Aw, c'mon,' I told him. 'Do this little movie for me. No one will ever see it.' Well, it was the last movie he ever did. It got so much attention that it made him famous. I think it freaked him out. Still, through it all, he was very eager to please. He was a very nice guy, very charming. And so handsome. The whole experience just clicked for us. It looked good on the screen, the story was good, the sets were good, Sky Dawson was wonderful. It was exhilarating."

This giddy sense of well-being was soon to be tempered by some harsh business realities. "We opened in New York, all set to make a fortune, but it wasn't meant to be. They charged an exorbitant rental for the theater, advertising was horrendously expensive, and they had very creative bookkeeping, so we made something like 25 dollars a week."

To make things worse, Drew and Richard had again sold video rights to Le Salon, and that company was raking it in hand over fist. Le Salon had approached Surge and offered to put up the production money in return for exclusive rights to the video distribution. Surge would still have the movie rights and the magazine franchise, so the guys eagerly agreed. "It seemed with every movie I was making, I was learning a lesson. And in every movie, it was a different lesson. I've made 21 movies now [1990], and I've been fucked 21 times." Drew and Richard never sold their video rights again.

In August 1982 the first Gay Games was staged, in San Francisco. Organized by former Olympic athlete Dr. Tom Waddell, the games brought hundreds of taut, well-muscled bodies together to display the athletic prowess of gays and lesbians to the world. It was staged as a celebration of gay power. It was the last hurrah of unfettered innocence and optimism for many years to come.

When Drew and Sal Grasso got wind of the big doings in San Francisco, they were both intrigued. The opportunity to utilize all those gay athletes as the framework for an X-rated film was irresistible, so they packed up their video cameras and headed north. "We came to San Francisco with our equipment to film background, and Tom Waddell was very…let's just say that they saw Al Parker with a video camera, and they went ballistic."

Waddell, aware of the growing Parker legend and intent upon keeping the games squeaky-clean, wasn't the least bit amused. He had a vision for gay America—at least as far as his big event was concerned—and it didn't include wild sex on film. "They were afraid their image would be compromised, which, of course, we had every intention of doing. We weren't, however, going to single any actual participant out and film him jerking off, and we certainly weren't going to overstep our rights as far as what we could show. It was the pageantry we wanted."

Waddell and his fellow organizers were less than impressed by the good intentions of Drew and Sal. "They assigned goons to follow us around—24-hour-a-day-type goons who dogged our footsteps and literally stuck their hands in front of the camera when they didn't want us to film something."

In spite of these problems the film *Games* was a success. In what would become standard for Surge Studio productions, Drew would first find a star with great box-office appeal and build the film around him. "One of the things I wanted to do at Surge was *not* be the focal point of what was going on. After *Inches* it was always somebody else's picture. I wanted longevity in this business, and I didn't want overexposure. So with each film it was my idea to find the hottest person around at the time." In 1982 boyish blond Leo Ford, already an experienced porn superstar, was the man of the hour.

The film opens with a whimsical, somewhat surreal scene in which Al, in the guise of a photographer, is sucking a disembodied cock through a glory hole gouged into a man-size cardboard cutout. Al is interrupted by an urgent call to photograph the Gay Games, leaving the cock—which remains tantalizingly unidentified—behind. That small frustration is soon subsumed in a truly Olympian orgy of exuberant, imaginative sex, the Gay Games serving only as the slenderest of threads to bind the scenes together.

In addition to Leo Ford, Drew also convinced his buddy Winn Strickland to bring his alter ego Mike Davis out of retirement and to make his debut in a talking film. "I had tons of lines to speak," Davis told Robert Richards during an interview shortly after the film was released. "Drew forced me to speak in *Games*. Steve Scott, the director, was creating this scenario as he went along. There wasn't even a script—that would have been easy. It was more to the effect of 'Sit here and be distraught—cry or something.' "

As Drew told it, getting Mike back in the saddle was no easy task. "He was very reluctant to do it. He felt confident in still work and silent films, but he had a slight speech impediment that he was very self-conscious about. It was the kind of thing that wasn't even noticeable to anyone but him. Still, I had to really work to convince him that he was right for the film. None of us knew about it while the film was being made, but I don't think he was well at the time." Although Winn worked with Drew as a set designer on a number of Surge films, *Games* was his last screen appearance.

The sex scenes follow, one after another—some of them strangely truncated, as though director and producer couldn't decide where to focus their energies. Davis appears as a swim coach, seducing one of his star performers. Then Al, playing himself as sex star extraordinaire, picks up hitchhiker Russ Franklin. The pair couple in the back of a van—a Drew Okun–Richard Cole specialty in their private lives as well. After a short, intense session, Al erupts like Old Faithful.

The spotlight then turns to Leo Ford. After a brief scene with Mike Davis he is drugged by a nefarious swim team member, taken advantage of, involved in a motorcycle accident, and rushed to a hospital. Working at this hospital is a horny orderly who preps patients for surgery by climbing into bed with them and impaling himself on their tumescent cocks.

Meanwhile, in a cameo appearance as a Games official, Richard introduces Al to gorgeous Georgio Canali. "I'd seen him in, I think, a Nova film, and I had the hots for him." As Al interviews Canali, he fantasizes an extremely hot scene that takes place against a stark black background.

The sex unfolds in a leisurely fashion. First Al tops Canali, then takes his turn on the bottom. "*Games* was the first talkie I'd ever been fucked in. I think Georgio was opposed to the idea at first...but obviously it was something he wanted to do

too. We had a good time." Al's demeanor in this scene under-
mines his *Flashback* claim that he did not like to be the passive
partner in his sex scenes. More to the point, as he candidly
admitted, he didn't much care for Kip Noll. With Canali the
case is entirely different. He rolls over—literally—and looks
great doing it. The scene that follows, celebrating the intense
coupling of two beautiful males, is long and very hot. The
lighting emphasizes every well-toned muscle and makes the
skin of both men glow. Al is so involved in the action that he
shoots while being fucked. So much for being uncomfortable.

Back in the hospital room the games are playing on a TV in
the background, while the orderly makes his rounds, expertly
servicing his patients. Then for the finale, Al is back in the
action, taking photos of Ford, the championship swimmer.
The pair have a brief scene together, and the film comes to a
close. When it is all over the images that linger are of Al Parker,
not Leo Ford. Al with the cutout of a glory hole, Al with
Canali, even Al topping Ford. His screen presence was such
that he couldn't help but dominate the films he appeared in.

Shot concurrently with *Games,* the Surge Studio production
of Steve Scott's *Dangerous* has been lauded ever since by critics for its daring examination of public sex. In his review for
Manshots Dave Babbitt says *Dangerous* is "the only film which
attempts to explore the psychology of anonymous danger sex
without sacrificing any erotic heat. It is the ultimate glory-
hole movie."

"Strictly serendipity," Drew claimed. "We had decided to
film *Games* and *Dangerous* simultaneously. *Dangerous* was one
of the most successful movies Surge has ever done, and it was
filmed in one evening. Like I said, it was strictly serendipity."

Both Drew and Sal Grasso enjoyed tearoom sex and thought

an exploration of the scene would be interesting on film. "It lent itself to easy filming for people who wanted to be in a porn movie but who didn't want to have their faces shown. It was anonymous sex, which was the mode of the day. And I knew all these exhibitionist types who had huge dicks but didn't want to be identified. We made arrangements with a bathhouse that had a stall with a glory hole. It was literally the bathroom, and it was tiny. Luckily, Sal Grasso was very small, so we could get him, the actors, and the cameraman in there."

When pressed by interviewer Jerry Douglas, Drew did admit that the filming took a bit more than a single evening. "What happened was, we were supposed to have the bathhouse for 12 hours, but around midnight the owner got real cranky and wanted to go home. We'd contracted for the place for a certain amount of time, and we'd shot most of it when they threw us out. We ended up building a set that duplicated the toilet and finishing it in the studio."

Richard was featured in this film but not Drew—unless you count the anonymous cock (which was, in fact, Al Parker's famous appendage) that pops through the glory hole in the final scene. Richard played a businessman who was in for a quick bit of sex. He appeared opposite Rick Faulkner, one of Drew's favorite performers. "His forte was incredible come shots." Reviewer Dave Babbitt agreed with Drew's assessment of Faulkner's talents. "This vignette"—in which he fucks Richard through a glory hole—"contains what many feel is the greatest come shot ever captured on celluloid. Richard slides his ass off Faulkner's dick just in time for an eruption worthy of Mount St. Helens. Faulkner's dick bounces like a springboard as it squirts quarts of juice high in the air."

Faulkner performs another scene in a phone booth, jerking off while talking on the phone to Chris Burns, who is cram-

ming a succession of ever-larger dildos up his ass. "We had
everyone convinced that the phone booth was really in a public place," Drew told Jerry Douglas. "We filmed him talking in
a real phone booth on a busy street, then finished the scene in
the studio."

There was also an autofellatio scene in the film, which was
always one of Drew's particular fetishes. "I've always been big
on autofellatio. It's always been one of the things that I find
very erotic, so whenever I find somebody that can do it, I put
him in a film." (In this case, it was performer Dixon Hardy.) "I
think Surge Studio is the studio that put autofellatio on the
map. Until Scott Taylor did it, it was something that no one
did. At least not on film."

1983 was a big year for Surge releases. Its third was another
classic, *A Few Good Men,* starring Lee Ryder. The title came to
Drew from a bumper sticker he saw while driving around—"it
was too good a title to let it go by." It was the second production they shot in the auditorium at Mac's bathhouse: "That
fabulous room—we were able to make into anything we wanted to make it." This time, they made it into a fairly convincing
barracks and peopled it with a bevy of extremely hot men.

The star anchoring this production was Lee Ryder, a well-
hung hunk who had caught Drew's wandering eye. After an
offscreen audition Drew decided he liked Ryder. "He was
much easier to work with than I thought he was going to be—
I had heard that he was difficult. He was certainly not difficult
on this film." Peter Barrie, the man who played the sergeant,
was also a man Drew very much wanted. "He had a fabulous
body. He's an executive with a track-lighting company, and it
was another one of those cases where I convinced him that
nobody would ever see the film. I don't mean to do these things

to people, but when they step in front of my camera their lives change. Nobody even knew he was gay, and all of a sudden, everybody knew. It made his life a nightmare."

Every scene in *A Few Good Men* delivers on all levels. The performers are sexy and enthusiastic, and the setups work to create considerable heat. The film opens with a new recruit in a chair getting his head shaved. His hair is peeled away, then a huge cock appears, waving back and forth in front of his face. He leans forward and sucks. We never see anything on-screen but mouth and cock, yet the scene is incredibly satisfying.

Subsequent scenes feature a coupling in a barn with two guys and several bales of hay; Ryder on a lower bunk, servicing a big, uncut cock that pokes through a hole in the mattress above him; a private on KP duty servicing his sergeant; a doctor administering rectal exams to five new recruits; an MP (horse-hung Michael Christopher) picking up an AWOL recruit, then working him over, top to bottom; and, finally, a hot scene between new recruit Ryder and sergeant Barrie.

The gimmick that was used to tie the scenes together, cementing fantasy and reality, was a fog machine. "It's terrible stuff that they use to keep mosquitoes away, and it's not conducive for anything. We only used it because we didn't have money to do dissolves"—an expensive editing procedure that fades one scene into the next. "It was just a lot cheaper and easier to rent a fog machine for $30 and dissolve with insecticide fog."

Although Surge did strive for professional effects, ultimately it was a very small company. "People are amazed when they find out that Surge was basically two people: my lover, Richard; and me. We were no MGM or Warner Brothers. All our sets were built in our living room in the house at Hermosa Beach. If you pulled back my carpets, my floors were ruined.

There were nail holes everywhere. We trashed that house—that house was our studio. All of our successful films, from *One in a Billion* to *High Tech,* were done in that house." All those films—significantly—were done without the participation of Sal Grasso.

CHAPTER FOURTEEN

Surge, After Steve Scott

In June 1983 Drew and Richard decided to take a vacation. They had three new feature films in release and needed some time off. They contacted their good friend and business associate, Sal Grasso, loaded up their new van, and took off cross-country. Drew, still enamored of his video camera, brought it along for the journey, taping everything that caught his eye along the way.

Also accompanying them as a part of their entourage was a puppy named Doogie. This little buff-and-white pooch would become their constant companion and would later provide solace for Drew after Richard's death. Doogie, billed as The Amazing Wonder Dog, was occasionally featured as a player in Surge's productions.

The travelers set out on the morning of June 1, 1983. One of the revelations of these private tapes is just how ordinary and domestic the daily life of the man so many lusted after really was. While on holiday Drew spent his private life playing with the dog, cruising, and squabbling with Richard over where to stop for the cheapest gas.

Along the way to Chicago they stopped off to visit friends in Arizona, toured the Truman library in Independence, Mo.—which they only located after a heated domestic tiff centering around Richard's disinclination to ask for directions—and visited Lincoln's home and the Illinois state capitol, both in Springfield. Through all the tours they listened attentively as good gay tourists are wont to do, hanging back from the body of the group to whisper catty asides to one another.

After dropping Sal Grasso off at a hotel on Chicago's Lakeshore Drive, Drew and Richard pointed the van south and headed to Florida. They hit all the usual tourist stops—Miami Beach, the Kennedy Space Center, Key West, and the Everglades. They sang along with the radio, carped about the rainy weather, took time out to pull off the highway for a swim, and cruised the boys. "Take a look at the ass on that one," Drew quipped to Richard. "Careful," Richard retorted. "He barely looks 18. You want to get yourself busted?"

Busted for cruising? Not exactly. Drew expended miles of videotape scanning the streets of towns and cities they drove through, checking out the local talent, but that wasn't what Richard was talking about. Robert Richards put it to me quite directly: "Those trips they took were sex trips. They went cross-country in the bouncing van. There are several scenes in Drew's movies that deal with sex in vans. It was no coincidence. The two of them were constantly picking up young men on their trips and fucking them in the back of the van."

That explanation went a long way toward elucidating the matter of the bed in the back of the van, often visible in Drew's videotapes. My first thought was that they had stayed in the van at night to save money, but that was complicated by the fact that Drew was always photographing Richard, naked, in various motel rooms. The setup seemed a little elaborate for Doogie, so what were they using it for?

Carl Simmons didn't know anything about porn films or an actor by the name of Al Parker, but he'll never forget the day that navy-blue van pulled up beside him. "I was walking back to my pickup. I'd been checking fence on some of my father's pasturage. We'd been having trouble with our stock getting out on the highway. Anyhow, my mind was about a million miles away. I didn't even know anyone was in the vicinity till he pulled up beside me and rolled down the window.

"This really handsome guy with a beard was smiling at me. There was another guy in the van—older, also bearded and good-looking. The driver asked if he was headed in the right direction for Kansas City. It seemed like an odd question, considering it was a state highway with road signs all over the place, but I told him he was about 70 miles from where he wanted to be.

"We started shooting the shit, and he asked me if I was up for a little fun. Well, I was, but I would've never had the nerve to go for it on my own. I nodded and got in the van. The guy behind the wheel offered me a pipe, and I took a hit. I'd heard of grass, but I'd never tried it. Within minutes I was flying high. The three of us got naked and did it right there on the side of the road. I was in the middle, like the meat in a sandwich. They were both really hot guys, wild as hell."

Carl emerged a while later, and the van drove off down the highway. "For the longest time, I just figured I'd happened upon a couple of hot guys. Then years later I met this guy who was into porn. He liked to watch videos while we were getting it on. One night he had one starring Al Parker. I sat up in bed and stared at the screen, totally blown away. I told my friend about it, and he was skeptical, to say the least. I don't think I ever really convinced him I was telling the truth."

Other men in other locales were enticed into the van by the horny pair's winning ways. New York businessman Kevin F. was far from a wide-eyed innocent when he crossed paths with them in Key West. "I actually went to the 55th Street Playhouse with a group of my buddies and saw Al Parker in person when he was promoting *Inches*. At the time, I remember being impressed that he had brains as well as a monster cock.

"I was out cruising the streets of Key West when this van caught my eye. It wasn't the van, actually—I don't know one car from another—but the activity around it. It was pulled up on a side street, in the shade of a big tree. This good-looking redhead I'd had my eye on back on Duval Street stuck his head in the open sliding door on the passenger side, then disappeared. About a minute later there was another fellow who approached from the other end of the street. He glanced in the van, did a double take, then walked over to the door. Damned if he didn't get in as well.

"By now my curiosity was getting the better of me. I turned and walked right up to the van. By this time it was rocking—quite literally. I stuck my head in and saw that there was a regular orgy going on. The place was fitted out with a bed in the back, and four naked guys were going at it. One of them saw me and motioned me in. I joined the fray, of course. About five minutes into it I looked down and recognized the guy who was blowing me.

" 'You're Al Parker,' I blurted. He didn't even miss a beat. He looked up at me and winked, then went right on sucking me off. Well, believe me, I wasn't about to miss a chance like that. I wrestled my way around to a sixty-nine position and got busy on that famous meat of his. It looked just as big in person as it did on the screen.

"Later that night I was telling someone about my adventure, and he just shook his head. 'Listen,' he told me, 'practically the entire population of Key West has been in that van. I heard one guy say he'd personally watched Parker and his pal suck off 20 guys. They just don't know when to quit.' Maybe so, but they were damned good at it."

Drew and Richard enjoyed their time in Key West. The tapes recorded the pair as they trolled up and down the narrow streets, cruising the local talent while Drew ogled them through the camera's lens. The sound track captured their evaluations of the bars they were in the previous night and their plan of attack for the upcoming evening's activities. They were clearly having a grand and glorious time, doing their best to lay the entire male population of the city.

Their odyssey continued, back up through Florida. Drew, tiring of the sameness of South Florida scenery, turned to Richard, who was driving naked. Drew panned his lover's toned body with the camera, lingering over shots of cock. The pair shared a pipe of marijuana, passing it back and forth across the console. Drew panned back to Richard a few minutes later, catching him with hard cock in hand as the van rolled north.

While driving through the Everglades, they stopped off to see the alligators. For this outing Richard was behind the camera. Drew was wearing the combat fatigues that Lee Ryder had filled so well in *A Few Good Men*. He and Drew were the same size, so Drew had commandeered them from Surge's wardrobe collection; they remained a favorite costume for the rest of his life. Drew led the tour, shirtless, looking very delectable. The two men bantered back and forth with each other, talking about what they were seeing, pointing things out to each other. Drew clowned for the camera, assuming different voices as he pretended to be both tour guide and tourist.

After stopping in Tampa to visit friends they pressed on, making a quick side trip to Disney World and Epcot Center. Drew loved Disney and filled the video sound track with his Donald Duck imitation right up to the gates of the park. He took no pictures inside, so we don't know if anything interesting happened during this particular visit, although Drew did have a checkered history with the folks who brought us Mickey Mouse.

Keith Reiter, Drew's long-time friend, business associate, and eventual life-partner, recalled one of Drew's escapades in Anaheim. "Drew had gone to Disneyland to show some people around. He sent them off to ride the rides, then set off on his own. This led to an encounter with a horny young man, which in turn led to some alfresco sex. Bottom line: Drew got caught sucking cock in the shrubs at America's number 1 family-entertainment destination. The guards hauled him and his partner in crime off to the jail on the premises. The most memorable part of the experience, to hear Drew tell it, was to look around at the walls of the holding cell and see framed pictures of Mickey, Goofy, and other cartoon characters dressed in Keystone Kop uniforms. He was thrown out and told never to come back. Of course, he went back every time he got the chance."

After Florida the guys headed west to New Orleans, camera rolling. There, they were subjected to the irritations of attempting to drive through the French Quarter. Drew taped street scene after street scene while Richard got crankier and crankier about the parking situation. After a brief stay in the city—from the evidence on the tape, they may never have found parking—they wended their way through Texas, stopping to visit a friend in Houston. Drew celebrated his 31st birthday in San Antonio on June 25, and a few days later the pair pulled up in front of the house at Hermosa Beach, tired but happy.

Shortly after their return a problem that had been festering with Sal Grasso came to a head. Sal had been the artistic force behind Drew's success in *Inches* and *Wanted* and had been around to assist with the birth of Surge Studio. Drew thought of Sal as an employee who should be paid a generous salary. Sal saw himself as deserving of partner status, entitled to a share of the profits. Drew balked. Sal sued. "The rift with Sal Grasso had to do with money," Jerry Douglas recalled. "They were very close friends, then they became super-enemies. After the blowup Drew had nothing but ugly things to say about Sal. He was furious."

"There was a terrible falling-out," Robert Richards confirmed. "Drew wanted all the subsidiary rights to the films, but Sal wouldn't give them to him. In Drew's eyes he was the producer, and Sal was a salaried employee. Sal didn't see it that way. Once the rift occurred, that was the end of it. Drew was done with him."

Not quite. Keith Reiter saw the dark underside of their falling-out. "I was driving through West Hollywood with Drew one day when Sal passed us. Drew saw him and suddenly looked like he'd been possessed by the devil. He floored the van and gave chase till we lost him in rush-hour traffic. It was an unsettling experience."

Now Drew was now on his own, and Surge would sink or swim based on his talent and diligence. He felt ready to meet whatever challenges lay ahead. "At that point I felt very confident about directing and editing. I had taken my lessons well."

For his first totally independent foray into filmmaking he chose Dave Connors, one of those huge-cocked specimens that

Drew consistently managed to find for his films. He also recruited his friend Winn Strickland to work on the physical aspects of the production.

One in a Billion is distinguished primarily by the fact that the sex scenes are set in unusual locations. Most memorable is the elevator scene. Here, Connors and costar Glenn Steers couple in a glass elevator on the side of a building.

"The elevator scene was thanks to Winn, who was already very ill. He had been diagnosed with AIDS in 1983, shortly after he appeared in *Games*. He suffered from Kaposi's sarcoma internally. I really believe that his creative work is what kept him alive. At that point, they didn't know what to do about Kaposi's, so they were giving him massive doses of chemotherapy. It was like battery acid to him. And still he kept on doing these sets for Surge. I really and truly think it was the work that kept him going."

The outdoor shots for the project were filmed in West Hollywood at a building on the corner of La Cienega and Sunset boulevards. "What happened was, we went to that building, with its glass front, and we did the exterior shots there. Then Winn recreated the elevator in the studio at Hermosa Beach, right down to the wallpaper. He was brilliant."

After an over-the-credits jerk-off scene, Connors boards the glass elevator with costar Glenn Steers. On the way up Connors gets his ass plowed. "Dave Connors did not want to get fucked in that movie. Glenn Steers, however—once he found out that Dave didn't want to get fucked—well, his dick just got harder and harder and harder. Glenn carried the day, and Dave gets his lights fucked out."

After the elevator scene, businessman Connors goes to his office, where he mounts an attack on Drew's *Games* costar, Sergio Canali, screwing him on top of his desk. The next scene takes place in a car wash with Connors and Jason Hill. "For this we went to a local car wash, and I said I was doing a student project. I told them it was a spy film and that supposedly the microfilm was going to be passed while these two guys were going through the car wash. The owner of the car wash was *thrilled* to help out the poor students with their film. I had to send my truck through that car wash eight times. We sent it through so many times that the starter was ruined. We got finished with the filming, and the starter wouldn't do its thing—that's how wet it was. I mean, that was the longest car wash in history. Then we went to my garage. I took a rod, and I hung strips of sponge off it, like they had in the car wash. Then I literally stood there moving this thing back and forth with a light in front of it so I could finish up the scene. Ah, the magic of film." The final scene features Connors in a very convincing three-way with a couple of horny TV repairmen in the bathroom.

One in a Billion was a huge success for Surge even though some critics carped about the pacing of certain scenes and the murky lighting in others. When it was all over, Drew and Richard breathed a sigh of relief. They had taken it to the next level, and Surge Studio was now their exclusive baby.

Their next film grew out of a trip that Drew and Richard took with their friend Winn on June 23–24, 1984. It was a typical road trip for them—Richard behind the wheel, Drew with his camera trained out the window, Winn ensconced in the back, and Doogie bouncing around all over the place like a slightly out-of-control beach ball.

The scenario played itself out in typical fashion, with Drew and Richard—just a couple of regular guys—out with their dog and a good buddy, enjoying nature and the open road. As was always the case, an easy, unforced domesticity reigned.

The trio wended its way up into the mountains on the way to a favorite campsite of long standing. As soon as they arrived they settled in for the night. Drew, the officially designated keeper of the fire, busied himself with starting a blaze while the others searched for dry kindling. "Just a campfire girl at heart," Drew quipped to the camera, carrying on just like any gay boy worth his Levi's. As night fell, they brought out the pipe and toked up while the fire burned down.

The underlying purpose of this jaunt was to scope out a locale for an outdoor picture. All the earlier Surge Studio productions had been shot indoors under studio lighting, and Drew felt it was time for a change of pace. "*Rangers* was serendipity," Drew told interviewer Jerry Douglas, employing one of his favorite words to explain the origins of the film. "Richard and Winn and I were literally out in the middle of nowhere when a pair of rangers came by and said, 'Don't drive on the roads tonight, because there's a road rally coming through here.' Well, we based our whole story on those two rangers who were going around telling people to steer clear of this big road rally." The private video shows Drew at work dashing up and down the roads to get footage, which he later used to weave the sex scenes together. "I had my video camera with me, and I shot the shit out of that road rally."

Nick Rogers and Chris West, as the rangers, are considerably more active than the pair Drew encountered on the mountain. They pop around their part of the Sierras spying on campers and emulating their horny antics. Al Parker puts in an appearance, playing the part of a lumberjack who gets involved in a three-way with Daniel Holt and Chris Allen. The scene is made memorable when Al ties his cock and balls together with Daniel Holt's rather formidable genitals to create what the

Bijou Video Catalog refers to colorfully as a "large, balled mess of man meat."

The film was another hit for Surge, a triumph marred for Drew when one of the stars committed suicide just days after the shoot was completed. "Chris West was this really hot blond guy who starred as one of the rangers. He made the film a success. He didn't have the biggest dick in the world, but he was truly a nice guy, and I could see him becoming a very big star. I don't know what the thing was with him, but I do know that it was very important to him to make this movie. Then right after he completed the filming—just days after—he got into a bathtub and slit his wrists. And that was that."

Beginning with *Rangers* and continuing for the next eight feature films, Drew engaged the services of Brian King as cameraman and Ted Sawicki as audio technician. These men were the founders of Jaguar, the pioneering gay-film production company whose 1971 film *The Experiment* was the first gay-porn film in which the performers actually emoted and spoke scripted dialogue. "When the film opened at the Park Miller Theater in New York in 1971, the owners called us up in a panic," Sawicki revealed in a recent interview. " 'I've watched five minutes of this thing, and there's no sex,' he complained. 'It'll never work.' Actually, there was no sex until almost a half-hour into the film, so by the time it came, the audience was involved with the characters and clamoring for them to get it on. The film played to packed houses at 20 bucks a ticket."

King and Sawicki had first encountered Drew back in 1979 during the filming of *Inches*. They were introduced by Sal Grasso. "We used to call Sal 'The Little Colonel,' " Sawicki recalled with a chuckle. "Every time we'd set up the lighting for a scene, Sal would stalk through—all 5 foot 5 of him—and

turn about half of them off. He was very into gloom in his productions." They worked with Drew on several of the productions he did for Sal, then reconnected with him for *Rangers.*

"The scenario for shooting was always the same," King said.
"We'd go to the Hermosa Beach house on Friday afternoon.
The shoot would begin on Friday evening and would be
wrapped up by Sunday afternoon. It was like a miniversion of
MGM studios. We always worked on film, not on video. We
had an allotted amount of footage for each film. Period. We'd
usually shoot five scenes, each one of which was carefully timed
and scripted. We knew how many rolls of film we had available
for each scene, and we'd crank it out. There were two cameras,
and we had very little waste."

The Hermosa Beach house-studio was a beehive of activity
during these weekends. "We'd be shooting upstairs, and Winn
Strickland would be in the basement making sets for the next
scene. Once our scene upstairs was finished, we'd move down
and start all over again. Winn was a genius, working quickly to
great effect.

"When Drew performed, he'd move from one side of the
camera to the other without a hitch. One minute he'd be
directing, the next he'd be screwing some guy's brains out. He
could ignore the camera crew completely and become totally
immersed in what was going on at the moment. He was a consummate exhibitionist—he had no inhibitions at all. Richard
would be right in there, taking the stills."

After these marathon weekends there would still be weeks of
work ahead—editing the rough footage and creating the finished product. Ted and Brian helped with the editing. "It was
a tedious job," Ted related. "This was film, not video. We edited the rough cut and got it the way Drew wanted it, then we'd
turn it over to two women who cut the negatives. Afterward,

Drew would transfer the negatives to make the video master. It had to end up on video because there was no longer a market for commercially released films. The work was done on about a half million dollars worth of equipment, which gave his films such a rich finish."

Working so close for so long, both men had a real opportunity to observe Drew. "He was extremely easygoing," Brian said. "He never once lost his temper or threw a silly queen tantrum when things didn't go his way. He was organized and professional, and working with him was fun. We knew what we were doing, and we did it."

"The weekends of filming would be like some sort of mad house party," Ted recalled. "Scenes were being shot, sets were being built, people were popping in and out all the time." Aside from the single "star" talent whom Drew would recruit as a centerpiece for the film, most of the actors were friends of Drew and Richard. "Most of the performers were just guys who had been at little private sex parties at the Hermosa Beach house, getting it on as friends," Ted continued. "Most of them were great. However, there'd always be one person who had problems—it was too hot, it was too cold, the food wasn't good enough, his costar wasn't hot enough. Fortunately, these types were always in the minority, and everyone else just did what they were asked to do."

Neither man has any negative memories of Drew. "I never had a bad experience with Drew," Ted said. "I remember our times together as full of fun. They used to set up the sound equipment in the kitchen at the house. I was starving one night, so I got into the refrigerator and found a pan of brownies. I ate my fill, only to find out about half an hour later that they were laced with marijuana. Drew loved his dope. Well, I didn't know what was happening, and I started to panic. I ran into the living room and announced I was having a heart attack. Drew saw the pan of brownies on the counter and started to howl with laughter. Once I was convinced I wasn't going to die, I sat back and tried to get used to being high."

Both men basically remember Drew as a centered, fun-loving, extremely sexual guy. "Both Drew and Richard were voracious sexually. The house at Hermosa Beach, while very much their home, was ground zero for wild parties. There was always something going on there.

"They were also both very popular regulars at Mac's, the bathhouse where they filmed *Turned On*. Another of their hangouts was the 8709—this was a really notorious bathhouse in West Hollywood. It was one of those places that screened their customers—meaning you had to be really hot just to get in. Drew and Richard were swingers," Ted recalled.

"When they weren't at home, they took their sex show on the road. Once Surge Studio started to make a profit, they always had a van that Drew and Richard would use to make trips cross-country and up and down the coast. Every time they bought a new one, Drew would make what he referred to as one of his 'conversions,' which meant that he was putting a nice bed in the back so he'd have a place to make it with the guys he was always out cruising around for.

"Drew was always on the lookout for sex. He was always stopping for hitchhikers—good-looking ones, that is. They provided a steady source of entertainment for him. He'd stop and pick them up. The guys might recognize him, or they might just be seduced by the handsome young man with the nice van and the little dog."

More of Drew's trademark humor emerges in the naming of his beloved pet. The dog's name, Doogie, was also one of the terms that Drew and his circle of friends used as slang for *penis.* "It was their term of choice," Ted recalled. "They were constantly referring to some guy as having a 'big doogie' or some such."

And then there was that 1961 Buick Invicta. Drew was passionate about cars—had been since high school. Throughout his life he owned a succession of automobiles—none of them, to Ted Sawicki's way of thinking, more outrageous than the Invicta. "Drew gave it to me, and I'm still driving it. The car is a real hoot. It has a body style that's more or less bullet-shaped, and it's painted a rather jarring flesh color. It looks for all the world like a penis on wheels. I never get in it without smiling and thinking fondly of my good friend."

CHAPTER FIFTEEN

The Movie Mogul

Around the time *Rangers* was released, Drew encountered another of those people he met from time to time who would have a profound influence on his life and fortunes. "He was doing a benefit in San Francisco," Keith Reiter recalled. "I happened to go, and we met." Drew's memory of their meeting was considerably more intense. "I met Keith at the Leather Daddy's Boy contest in San Francisco, but I was so crazed that night that I wasn't aware of what was going on. When I emcee something, I'm just not there. Then one day Richard and I were in the Castro, and this guy walked across the street with this basket down to his knee, and I said, 'Jesus Christ, did you see that dick?' Anyway, Keith crossed the street and was gone. Then one night not long after, I was judging a contest at the Eagle in San Francisco, and the judges were all standing out front talking, and I saw this person walking toward me. I said, 'I have seen that before.' It's one you don't forget. Well, I made a point of meeting him, and we tentatively made a date to get together after the contest. Of course, I could hardly wait. After the fact, Keith told me that before we got together, he was thinking about breaking the date off —you know how it is: Now that he had me, he wasn't interested anymore. Fortunately, we decided to go ahead with the date."

The one thing both men were able to agree on was the fact that they liked each other a lot. "We clicked instantly," Reiter said, "and were best friends from the first moment. The following morning I met Richard, and we were like The Three Musketeers. We visited back and forth between Hermosa Beach and San Francisco all the time."

Reiter is the owner of the San Francisco Pump Works, producer of the vacuum penis pump that Drew featured in several of his later, safer-sex films. It was a product that attracted Drew instantly because of its promise to enlarge a man's penis. To Drew, the idea of making something big even bigger was irresistible. "I had played around with several apparatuses that promised to make your cock bigger, but this was the first time I'd ever seen one that really worked." It appealed directly to Drew's sense of the unusual. "Anything that is bizarre, I love. I am bent toward the bizarre. I'm not afraid to let people know that. I like things that are strange and different. I wanted to base a movie around the device."

While this seed was germinating, Surge had other projects already in the works. The next feature they produced was *Head Trips:* a story, as Drew put it, "of the fantasy machine that ate the quarters." The fantasy machine is actually a coin-operated peep machine that links the four scenes in the film. The first scene features a waiter and two businessmen who fuck in the middle of a busy restaurant. The restaurant was, of course, created in the Hermosa Beach studio by Drew's friend Winn. "He also built the fire truck used in the second scene. It was basically a piece of red plastic with some white tubing on it, but it looked incredible. It was another example of Winn's genius."

Al appears here—in spectacular form, as always—with Rydar Hanson. His enthusiasm for foreskin is showcased in their scene together as he mouths the man's enormous, uncut cock to great effect. In fact, most of the men in the cast are uncut, providing more evidence of Drew's personal hand in the casting of all Surge Studio productions.

He was developing a particular look for his Surge men. As he told Jerry Douglas, "There's always somebody that I want to use. Falcon Studios, Matt Sterling. Catalina, they really have the market sewed up on pretty preppy boys. And those filmmakers do what they do really well. I enjoy their films, but I'm aiming my films for men who enjoy men as opposed to boys. My men are older, they're between 30 and 40. I wouldn't be opposed to casting a man who's 50, just so long as he was hot."

The next Surge production, *Therapy,* was built around a psychiatrist, played by Daniel Holt. "I went to research some sort of problem that the patients in the film could have. I threw the book I was reading open on the floor, the pages parted, and I saw the words CASANOVA COMPLEX. You know, I think psychiatrists are full of shit. I think they have more problems than anyone else. So, anyway, I decided this psychiatrist would tell all his patients that they've got a 'Casanova complex.' Holt's father is a shrink," Drew concluded with wry satisfaction.

Holt's character serves as a springboard for the action. He gets off through the sexual exploits of his patients. The doctor listens to tales of tearoom sex, alley sex, self-abuse by a muscle-bound blond stud who jerks off in front of a mirror, and a Walter Mitty-esque fantasy of a fellow who wins the lottery and then screws the bank manager in a vault full of gold bullion.

Drew was particularly pleased with Rex, the man he had chosen to play the muscle stud. Rex had been the discovery of Nova, a rival studio who had paid him a huge chunk of change to star in one of its productions. Ted Sawicki remembered vividly Drew's excitement over stealing him away—and at a discount. "Drew was ecstatic that he had gotten Rex for less than other studios were paying. He couldn't help himself—he boasted about saving all that cash every chance he got."

The response to *Therapy* was mixed. The critics found the plot too predictable and the sex too tepid. In comparison to other Surge productions this film seemed lackluster and tame. Could it be that Al Parker was losing his Midas touch? Or was it perhaps that he just needed to shift gears and follow his instincts?

Ever since Drew had met the monumentally endowed Keith Reiter, he had been intrigued with the idea of using the vacuum pumps in a feature film. As he got ready to put *Strange Places, Strange Things* into production, he decided to take the plunge. "That film was the first time we used the vacuum pump. That scene, which was done with Ivan (Keith Reiter's stage name) and Scott Taylor, was the best scene in the movie. I convinced Ivan to do it, over his strenuous protests. He had this wonderful pump mechanism and one of the biggest dicks I've ever seen in my life.

"We knew that Scott Taylor was into this stuff, so we were able to get him too. Scott had a flexible tube that flattened his dick as well as pumped it up. It's called a Beaver Tail, and it was another example of Scott being magnificently crazy and erotically inventive."

The scene was a highlight in a film most reviewers agreed represented Al Parker at the peak of his form behind the camera. Reviewers were amazed by what the well-hung pair was able to do with a vacuum pump to, in the words on one enthusiastic critic, "enlarge their meat and balls to distorted proportions, then bend over and conduct a double self-suck session." In the scene Taylor also goes down on Reiter. "He hated me for that," Reiter confided. "He hated me because he was captured on film going down on a big, pumped-up cock. He hated the scene, and he hated me. He didn't want people to know whether he was straight or gay."

Other scenes include a hot coupling in a dirty underground utility tunnel; a session on a doctor's examination table in which a foreskinned man is talked out of circumcision by a comprehensive display of all the things one can do with Drew's favorite little skin sleeve; and a scene on a scaffolding high above Hollywood Boulevard that unfolds while people watch from below.

Scott Taylor had another idea for a scene in the film, an idea which he prefaced by telling Drew, "There's something I want to do on film, but I don't want to tell you what it is beforehand." Drew turned him down. "I knew he was capable of doing anything, and I sure as hell didn't want to go to jail." Drew confided in Jerry Douglas that he shot the scene anyway, but didn't use it because "it was just so disturbing. I figured somebody down in Florida or somewhere would get hold of this and prosecute, and I'd be in jail for 100 years."

Keith Reiter, who wasn't as enamored of Scott Taylor as Drew was, told me what Jerry Douglas and Drew held back from their interview. The scene Taylor wanted Drew to film was beyond the pale. "Scott would be standing in an all-white room and he would cut his foreskin with a razor, spattering his blood around the pristine space. He had also done this onstage a couple of times. It was grotesque." Clearly this was an act not destined for prime time, but it was one which piqued the part of Drew that craved what was bizarre, strange, and outré.

"What served Scott on the stage didn't work for him so well in life," Keith continued. "He fancied himself a performance artist. During some of his staged sex shows he would gag himself on stage and vomit on the audience. He was always on the verge of being on the streets. He always had some far-fetched project he wanted Drew to work on with him. Once he came to our house for dinner and described a scenario wherein he and another person would break into someone's home, prepare dinner from what they found in the house, then leave it for the person when he came home. Drew was intrigued by the concept, but nothing ever came of it because Scott was so domineering. He wanted complete artistic control."

Hard Disk Drive was the next Surge project, and it was only a partial success. "It was probably my least favorite film. I'm not saying it was a bad film, just that we had something completely different planned. We had a location all scouted out but lost access to it a day before the filming began. Lucky for us, we had Winn Strickland to make the sets. His sets were wonderful, very surrealistic. It was a very stylish movie, sort of a sequel to *Head Trips,* and I'm not one to do sequels."

The gay-video critics weren't kind to *Hard Disk Drive,* berating Drew for uneven directing and inattention to detail. The film opens with a clever courtroom scene, played out against a backdrop of Winn's cartoon cardboard cutouts of jurors. The sex is intense. The camera work is dynamic and to the point. The final scene, set in a motel room with voyeurism as a plot device, is also well-filmed, the camera catching all the nuances of the intense sexual action. The action in the middle of the film flags, however, which led one reviewer to excoriate Drew for "creating tedious sex loops with jumbled editing and sub-standard camera work."

Part of the problem was that Drew and Richard were trying to do too much, too quickly, and it was beginning to show. Drew realized that Surge Studio was in danger of producing too much of a good thing. "What I was finding was that by doing movies so quickly, by the time the publicity builds up on one movie you've already released another, and they were overlapping to the point where I was doing too much, too fast. Not that they were bad movies or that they didn't do well. It was just that the pace we'd set for ourselves was not realistic."

Perhaps stung by the buzz in the reviews that he might be losing his touch, Drew's next project was quite ambitious. The plot centered around the collapse of a mine shaft. The set for *Century Mining* was "the most spectacular thing that anybody's ever built for one of these films," Drew claimed in an interview. "It set the standard. It was a completely collapsing set. I have tapes of that set from the beginning of the building of it in an empty room to the final scene where it caves in."

The creation of this particular set was especially poignant because it was the last set Winn Strickland constructed before his death. He was desperately ill, literally "dissolving before our eyes," as Drew later recalled. "He put the set together in 72 hours. It was phenomenal. Just phenomenal. At that point he couldn't walk, and he weighed maybe 125 pounds."

Short on plot, *Century Mining* is long on what counts in a successful Surge production: "Foreskin; large cocks; lustful, masculine men; and incredible sucking and fucking," as one reviewer put it. One of the best scenes in the film is interracial, between black actor Ray Williams and white actor Case Hardin. Drew was one of the first directors to use black men in his films. "Blacks in these movies were virtually taboo, for whatever reason. I think blacks are very attractive, erotic, and exotic."

He was also intrigued by the stereotype of the black male as hung bigger than his Caucasian counterpart. "Drew was always searching for big cocks," Robert Richards said. "Drew was fascinated by dick. It wasn't so much the sex he wanted as it was to see the sex organs of his partner. When he'd talk about someone, he'd always mention their penis size in the first sentence. It ran through everything he did.

"This quest for huge cocks led him to black men. One time I took him to a club called 12 West, on the waterfront on New York City's West Side. Drew wanted to go, and so I took him. I got him in and then left. The next morning he called me and was ecstatic. After I left he found a young black guy who was a conservative-looking bank teller, who just happened to have a 14-inch cock. Drew was absolutely thrilled by this fact."

His friend Keith Reiter mentioned another occasion when a large black penis intervened in Drew's life, this time separating him from his beloved dog. "Drew was up in Griffith Park (a well-known Los Angeles gay cruise spot) with Doogie. Doogie was off-leash and running around when Drew, cruising as always, wandered off into the bushes and found a big black cock to suck on. Doogie ran off. Afterward, Drew was distraught. He put up posters all over the park and the surrounding neighborhoods, offering a reward for the dog. After about three days he actually recovered the pooch." Doogie wasn't very happy with his owner for this lapse. "When he arrived at the house where Doogie was being kept, Doogie snarled at him when he first saw him."

The critics, however, weren't snarling about *Century Mining*. They liked the interracial sex and the raw intensity exhibited by the performers. They praised every aspect of the production, calling it an "ambitious endeavor that succeeds all around." Obviously, Al Parker the director had hit his stride again.

In spite of Drew's thoughts about slowing down, Surge was still cranking out films on a regular basis. Next in line was a road picture—a trucker picture, to be exact. Drew had always wanted to do a picture focusing on that most masculine of fantasies—18-wheelers and the men who jockeyed them on the highways. He admitted that the Gage Brothers film *Kansas City Trucking Co.* "was a very good idea." Perhaps it was also a chance to kick a little sand in the faces of those very successful producers and directors of gay porn. "Drew seemed to have a resentment against the Gage Brothers," Robert Richards told me. "I don't know any of the details, but he spoke of them in a very negative way. I suspect it was because he couldn't cut a deal with them to make a film together."

Whatever the case, *Oversize Load* was another of Surge Studio's instant classics. "I was traveling on the highway one day behind a truck that had a banner that said 'Oversize Load.' As with many of my pictures, I start out with the title. The title is the premise, and the premise builds into a story, and that's how it comes about."

This time the star Drew built the film around was Scott O'Hara. Drew was drawn to O'Hara because he was reputed to possess the biggest dick in San Francisco. Drew, self-admitted size queen that he was, couldn't resist. When he learned that O'Hara could also perform autofellatio, Drew was hooked. "I said to myself, 'I want to work with this guy.'"

O'Hara was delighted. In his autobiography, *Autopornography: A Memoir of Life in the Lust Lane,* he gives a detailed account of his experience. He met Drew in August

1985, when Drew was in San Francisco to judge a greasy-jockstrap contest at the Powerhouse bar on Folsom Street. O'Hara almost didn't enter because the rules stated that he couldn't bare his genitals, and he believed "his chest was nothing special." A little further meditation led him to change his mind. After all, a jockstrap contest was "crotch-oriented enough so that I figured I could win it. I also wanted to meet Al and hopefully be in one of his videos. I figured that if I were in an Al Parker video, I could count on some uncut dick, at the very least."

The big day arrived, and nobody wanted to enter the contest, so the prize was raised from $100 to $150. Three or four contestants were finally mustered, two of whom were twins. "Mr. Marcus, perpetual emcee at these events, poured motor oil all over the jockstraps, and we got to be as lewd and lascivious as we felt comfortable with, which meant that my dick *did* get exposed, and yes, I won.

"Al and I made the connection, he made the inevitable offer, and we scheduled the shoot for early September. The week before the shoot Al and his lover invited me down to spend the weekend at their house in Hermosa Beach. Oh, it was an official audition too, I suppose, but I was just enjoying myself. It's the only real casting-couch interview I've ever had: I spent the night sandwiched between the two of them—I've always liked sandwiches. I fucked Richard; Al did this pretzel number with his dick and my dick (tying their cocks together with a rawhide thong, a move he had perfected in the film *Rangers*), and eventually fucked me. A good time was had by all. And I was officially hired."

The following weekend was frantic and laid-back simultaneously. "Al knew how to get a good performance out of his actors: Don't tell them how to do their job—just turn them loose on each other and let them go to town. I was in three scenes." Every one, in fact, but the opening three-way, which featured Richard in his final screen appearance. "It all worked out OK. The scene in the can with the blond wasn't easy. I don't like to fuck standing up, and I wasn't turned on by the guy, even though he had a great ass.

"I have only one complaint, and I can't decide if it was deliberate sadism or accidental bad luck. Al had asked me what sort of partner would turn me on. I told him 'Dark-haired, dark-skinned, foreskinned, Mediterranean.' He got the picture because we shared similar tastes. He assured me that he had several such men on line for the production.

"And so he did. Two of them. He even put them in a scene with me. It was the final scene, when I was supposed to be standing at a washbasin, shaving [while] watching this scene unfold in the showers. I got to jerk off, watching—but never joining in. To this day, when I watch that scene I get hungry—and angry. A foreskin I was that close to but never tasted. A set of tattoos I saw but never licked. A pair of hairy calves that I would've loved to worship but didn't get the chance. God, that man knew how to tease."

One of those missed opportunities in the shower scene was Jeff Turk, who had costarred with Drew in the Falcon loop *Rocks and Hard Places* and in the legendary porn epic *The Other Side of Aspen*. "I had lost touch with him for years, then Richard and I were at a street fair in Los Angeles, and I saw this guy with a beautiful body, beautiful face, and it was Jeff. I was always very attracted to him and loved working with him. I think he's hot sex, and I asked him if he'd be interested in doing a picture. He hadn't done anything for years, but he said 'Yeah,' so I got him."

O'Hara may have been frustrated by the film, but the critics and audience were not. *Oversize Load* captured the freewheeling sexuality of the early '80s and garnered favorable comparisons with the Gage Brothers' classic trucker films Drew had been emulating. It is a classic fantasy wherein there are no limits to sexual possibilities. It is a world of perpetual summer, with nothing ahead but the open road. It is, in short, a paean to a way of life that had already ended.

High Tech, Surge's next project, marked an end and a beginning for Drew. It was the last film he would make with his lover of almost 14 years. It was also the first of the safer-sex films that were to become Surge Studio's trademark. "*High Tech* was Keith's creation," Drew told Jerry Douglas. "I told Keith to round up a group of guys who were really into it, and promised that I'd make them stars."

As the toll from the AIDS epidemic continued to climb, Drew had become increasingly interested in safer sex. "I thought, 'How much safer can you get than encasing your dick in lucite?'" Keith put out the call among his friends and clients, and several showed up at the house in Hermosa Beach. "We just put them against a simple black background and let them go at it."

The six guys featured in the film stand around admiring one another's monstrously large, pumped-up meat, but there is nothing in the way of real sex presented in the video except for a cocksucking scene which temporarily derails the safe-sex concept. The film offers pump aficionados and size queens a visual feast but is primarily a fetish film. The film has a certain grotesque appeal but, unlike the typical Surge feature, is not really a sex video. Still, it was a triumph for Drew. "Everyone said that *High Tech* was such a special film that no one would be interested, but the response was phenomenal. Still is."

CHAPTER SIXTEEN

Death, Grief, and Renewal

In the early months of 1986, as Winn Strickland's condition worsened, he moved in with Drew and Richard, and the two men took care of him until his death. According to friends, this quiet compassion was typical of Drew. At this point in the AIDS epidemic people weren't as understanding as they later became about the disease, often shunning its victims, pretending they didn't exist. While many gay men were left to spend their last days unattended in isolation wards, Winn was loved, well-cared for, and surrounded by his friends.

After *High Tech* was wrapped up Drew and Richard packed the van and headed north to Vancouver. Their ultimate destination was Expo, the World's Fair held in Vancouver during the spring and summer of 1986. The trip videos Drew always took during these jaunts are, as usual, full of scenery of all types. They are also, more than usually, full of images of Richard. Although he still looked wonderful, Richard was plagued by a hacking cough he couldn't shake. Drew alluded to the cough on several occasions, obviously irritated—perhaps terrified?—by its intrusion into their lives.

At one point, after Drew had stuck the camera's lens into Richard's face for the umpteenth time, Richard rather grumpily snapped, "You'll wish you had more pictures after I'm long gone." Drew responded in a frightened voice, "That isn't even funny. Don't say that."

They traveled up the coast, stopped off to visit friends in Seattle, then made their way north to Canada. After taking in the sights at Expo they turned again toward home, touring Mount St. Helens along the way. They stopped all along the route, reading plaques and taking photographs, rubbing elbows with the other tourists and sharing their sense of wonder at the power of the volcano.

Shortly after they got back home, Keith Reiter and a friend drove down from San Francisco to visit. "We all went down to Disneyland. Richard, who loved to drive, was behind the wheel as always. Then, on the way back that night, he didn't drive. It was my first clue that something was seriously wrong. He got home that night, got into bed, and never really got up again. He was ill for four months. We all thought he had mono."

Drew was desperate, but there was nothing he could do to help. "Richard just couldn't shake off the bronchial condition he'd picked up on our vacation. He'd always had a bad reaction to antibiotics, but he had to resort to taking them. I used to crush them into his food for him. Then, somehow, a small bit of one of the pills got lodged in his throat and burned a hole in his esophagus." (His throat, as you may recall, was a mass of scar tissue as a result of his childhood accident with the bleach.) "After that he was no longer able to eat or breathe properly."

In a panic Drew called Keith and asked him to come and be with him. "I didn't realize how close we really were till

Richard was dying and Drew called me and asked me to come down to be with him. Of all the people he knew, he asked for me to come."

The doctors did more tests and came to Drew with the bad news. "Finally, on Friday, out of the blue, he was diagnosed as having AIDS. The doctor predicted he had only three or four days to live. Four days later he died in my arms."

Drew was devastated. Richard had been there by his side since the beginning of his career. He was the business acumen behind Surge Studio. He was the rock that had anchored Drew's life for almost 14 years. "I had no time to prepare myself—not that any amount of time *would* have prepared me. I suppose it was better for Richard that it happened so fast. It's strange, but in most AIDS cases one lover dies and the other stays on, kind of lost, having to deal with first the sorrow and then the endless legal hassles."

Richard had never made a will, and the document Drew hastily scribbled for Richard to sign on his deathbed was later questioned by insurance companies and financial institutions. "Everyone should have a will," Drew raged to Robert Richards. "Even if someone is on his deathbed, he should try to make out a will, have three people witness it, and follow through on whatever steps are necessary to make it legal and binding. The next-of-kin claim is very strong and impossible to fight unless there is a very clear and legal will. You and your lover may have bought something together—like maybe Marilyn Monroe's report card—but now the relatives find out it's worth a lot of money, and they're going to fight to keep it, even if you bought it together. Gays are upwardly mobile, and people are interested in their property."

In addition to the grief and legal difficulties, there was the matter of Drew's sister's inexplicable behavior. "I have a sister who is a doctor," Drew told a TV audience during a 1988 appearance on Phil Donahue's talk show. "And now, seeing as how I was involved with someone who died of AIDS, she won't let me in her home any longer. She doesn't want me to be around her kids." Drew had always respected and looked up to Meg. Then, from nowhere, she became a raging homophobe. Robert Richards remembered it as "a breach that never quite healed." Janie was also at a loss. "I don't know what her problem was. Nobody could understand why she reacted the way she did. We all thought it was kind of screwed up. I mean, she was a doctor and should have known better."

Richard's death caused a total rupture in the fabric of Drew's life. Not only was his business partner and companion gone, his whole way of life no longer seemed viable. "I've sold the rights to all of my films," he told Robert Richards in an interview shortly after his lover's death. "I basically don't want to go on doing them. It's not fun anymore. It was better when I had someone to share it with."

Selling the films turned out to be like a chapter from *The Godfather*. Surge had produced ten films to which Drew had the rights. He loaded them up and took them to a big porn producer, who bought them for $10,000 each. The man who bought the tapes was a shady character who was later sent to prison for income tax evasion and jury tampering. "Drew had a great story to tell about it," Keith Reiter recalled. "As he sat in the office, the guy snapped his fingers and somebody appeared with a big bag of cash. Drew looked down and started to reach into the bag. 'Parker, you don't gots to count it,' the man told him. There was $100,000 in the bag, in small bills. Drew went right out and bought himself a '64 Corvette."

Even with his bag of cash and his fancy car, Drew was lost. All the things he had relied on and believed in were gone. He couldn't even look at pornography in the same way. "When I watch a porn film, I just keep counting the people in it who are dead. Sometimes, and this is very eerie, I find myself wondering if, perhaps, I'm watching the very moment when they got sick."

This morbid train of thought led him to excoriate the entire industry—which at the time was shamelessly ignoring the AIDS epidemic. Even as films were beginning to reflect safer-sex practices, Drew doubted the filmmakers' sincerity. "They will only change according to what the market demands but certainly not in any effort to make people's lives safer. Maybe someday, out of the kindness of his heart, some producer will only allow some sweet kid to get porked twice instead of three times in a film, but that's about as far as their humanitarian instincts will carry most of the people in this business."

Drew foundered in the aftermath of Richard's death. Dealing with the legal hassles he faced kept him busy and sane, but he was totally withdrawn from life. It was during this troubled time that Drew began to work on large-scale art pieces that consisted mainly of windows set in brick walls. "Drew did some fabulous artwork," Keith recalled. "He did what he called constructions. He'd go around to junk stores and collect windows from churches and warehouses, and he would construct sides of buildings with the windows. The pieces were created from brick and metal and downspouts. They looked for all the world like parts of real buildings. He once did an AIDS benefit, and they were shown at a private garden party in West Hollywood by a gentleman who was in business with Liz Taylor."

For a time, these pieces became something of an obsession. Even when he was away from the house in Hermosa Beach,

Drew was driven to express himself through these constructed pieces. "I remember once when he came to visit me when I was living in Ipswich, Massachusetts," Drew's father, Seymour, told me. "He picked up a stained-glass window from a church and built a wall around it. He called the piece 'Ipswich.' "

These constructions were primarily a way for Drew to deal with his depression as he worked his way through the grieving process. "All of my art has one theme in common: bricked-up windows." Drew told an interviewer. "I began doing it as a release after Richard died and I stopped making films. Bricked-up windows symbolized my feelings. The only purpose of a window is to be open; when it is bricked up, it is no good. Everybody has had a different idea about them. I liked that." Examples of his work are visible as backdrops in some of his later films, particularly in the scene from *Turbo Charge* where Drew seduces Justin Cade.

Through all of this Drew's friends stood by him, keeping a watchful eye on his activities. "Friends were kind, always calling and inviting me to dinner or to parties. Most of the time I said no, but fortunately they kept calling. One night the phone rang, and someone invited me out, and I accepted without hesitation. When I hung up, I realized that for the first time in 13½ years, I had accepted an invitation without first shouting, 'Hey, Richard, so-and-so wants us to come to dinner on Saturday. OK?' I had done something on my own. I guess that moment was the beginning of my new life."

Around this time Drew went back to New York City and met up with his old friend Robert Richards. The two conducted another in their series of interviews, and they got together for dinner. Even at this point in his life Drew hadn't lost his wicked sense of humor. "One night Drew called up and asked if I wanted to go to dinner. I had a young friend here with me who was intrigued by the possibility of meeting Al Parker. I asked if he could come along. Drew said yes, and we arranged a time.

"The young man was Sam Watters, who later became the coowner of *The Advocate*. Sam was very refined—tall, thin, and elegant. He was an art historian at heart. He had never been exposed to a porn star before, and he was overwhelmed by Drew's openness and his level of comfort with himself. He may have been a bit smitten by him. In any case, a day or so later, Sam asked me to get a photo of Drew for him, signed if possible.

"I called Drew, and he agreed. He said to me, 'Your friend seems really shy and uptight.' I told Drew he'd just been bowled over. Drew sent a picture over to Sam by messenger. It was a head shot of Drew, with an inscription: 'Dear Sam, take it to the balls. Love, Al Parker.' Sam was very disappointed because he would have liked to put it out on display, but the inscription was a little too direct for his social circle."

Drew and other members of the Hermosa Beach family had all been sensitized to their own mortality by Richard's death. "Right after Richard died Drew and Wolf and I bought a cabin in the woods, about 20 minutes out of Guerneville, in Northern California," across-the-alley neighbor Dean Myers said. "It was in a beautiful place and, at the time, was relatively inexpensive to operate. We bought it so that if anyone else in our group got sick, he'd have a place to go to and live out the rest of his life in peace and comfort. It gave us all a sense of security.

"We bought the place in '88 or '89. Shortly afterward I moved to Texas. Drew used it a lot for the first three years. I know that he spent a lot of time there."

Once reconnected to the land of the living, Drew forged ahead without looking back. In a very short time, he found someone who captured his attention. Justin Cade had recently broken up with his lover, Joe Cade (no relation), and found himself at loose ends. Justin had won second place in his weight class in bodybuilding at Gay Games II in San Francisco. He had also caught the discerning eye of porn performer Pierce Daniels. "Pierce wanted to meet me," Cade recalled. "We got together and he took me to L.A. He said he knew Al Parker and told me he'd introduce us."

The pair met, and something clicked for them. "We kind of hit it off right away. We were very compatible and instantly felt comfy with one another. I was getting ready to go back to Canada to visit my folks, and I gave Drew the number there. He called me and invited me to come to L.A. for Thanksgiving. I agreed to come, and we had a really great weekend. We discovered that we were sexually compatible and that we had other things in common as well. About a week after that Drew called and invited me down to Hermosa Beach for Christmas. I stayed the week. We came up to San Francisco for New Year's Eve. We went to a big party that night, then on New Year's Day we packed some stuff from my apartment, and I moved to Hermosa Beach. Shortly thereafter I quit my job cutting hair in San Francisco and closed up my apartment."

For his part, Drew felt some guilt about getting involved so soon, but at the same time he realized that he couldn't thrive alone. "At first I felt guilty that it was happening so soon after Richard's death, but what does the amount of time you spend waiting to get on with your life have to do with how much you loved a person? I've come to terms with the fact that Richard can't and won't be replaced—that whatever lies ahead for me won't be what I had with him. He was my first lover. I know I can't recapture that. I also realize that, for me, happiness means being with someone, and I'm very fortunate to be seeing someone now. Someone very nice."

Drew began to bounce back from the blow of Richard's death, gradually falling into his old entrepreneurial ways and managing to keep both himself and Justin busy. He initiated Justin into the joys of wallpaper removal, his old standby from the early days with Richard. "We went everywhere—even as far as Palm Springs—to remove wallpaper," Justin recalled. Drew also had his mail-order business, so we kept busy."

The mail order end, which had originally been confined to the Surge video collection, had been radically expanded shortly before Richard's death. Drew had sold off all rights to the videos for a bag of cash, but a much more lucrative venture had presented itself in the form of Keith Reiter and his pumps. "By the mid '80s the video business was changing," Keith told me. "Videos that had sold for $79 were going for $19 or less, and people were [duplicating] them rather than buying them. Drew's income was in danger of drying up." Drew needed the money, and Keith needed some good advertising. "Drew was never really a part of my business, but it was good for sales to make people think he was. He helped me in the business, working in production right alongside of me. He also put an ad for my pumps at the end of the film *Strange Places, Strange Things,* which was very nice of him."

The melding of Drew Okun with the vacuum cylinder was a business match made in marketing heaven. It was the perfect blending of man and machine, and it provided both him and Keith with a comfortable income. It was a device that catered to Drew's fantasies of big cocks, a machine that took a big dick and turned it into a monstrous, enormous dick. What could be better than that? "It is a true cult apparatus," Drew enthused to Jerry Douglas. "It has turned out to be something even bigger than the video company. There are now clubs that specialize in nothing but. There are magazines. Everybody always wants a bigger dick. Even as strange as my life has been, if you'd ever told me that I was going to end up as part of a company that made penis enlargers on a grand scale, I would've told you that you were crazy. But this is what happened."

Drew also began dabbling in real estate. He approached the subject recklessly—he had never had much of a head for business—but nonetheless he made a killing. "It's funny: When it seems like there's nothing to care about, you take chances you would never take in business if you're looking for a long-term future. I started to buy property, and lo and behold, it turned out to be a gold mine."

For all his vaunted cynicism, Drew couldn't stay away for long from the business that had been so successful for him. But he wasn't willing to return to what had come before. Rather, he had a vision of himself as a crusader who would eroticize safer sex and bring it to the public. "I saw that nobody was making films that were safe. There were no safe-sex films that I could see that were also erotic. There might be fucking with a rubber, but there was nothing erotic about it, and I felt I could eroticize safe sex. So I did."

In response to a question regarding how he felt he could fit into the pornography industry after the death of his lover–business partner from AIDS, he replied that he refused to be regarded as a pariah. "I'm not allowing myself to be categorized that way. Why am I different than all the other men who made films and were sexually active from the late '70s to the mid '80s? My experience has been the same as theirs—no better, no worse. We've all been exposed to the same things. As a matter of fact, I think that, used properly, my exposure and experience could now make me a powerful voice for safe sex."

Switzerland agreed with him. He was approached by the Swiss government and asked to make a safe-sex video that could be attached as a prologue to all gay-porn films. "It was to be much like a music video. I said I would do it, because I thought it was important." This move, although good for AIDS prevention, was not well-received by Drew's public. Keith Reiter recalled that it very nearly cost him his business. "People didn't want to see safe sex in a porn film. They didn't want to think about AIDS. He actually got a lot of nasty letters from people complaining about the safe sex shown in his later films."

In the short he made for the Swiss government, Drew pulled out all the stops and did everything he could to eroticize safety. There was cock sucking and fucking with condoms, rimming with Saran Wrap, finger-fucking with rubber gloves, and an Al Parker signature—what he called the pussy-dick trick, where he tied his cock and balls together to create a fucking hole. "Just like a pussy," he was fond of saying. "We do stuff with rubbers, and especially with Saran Wrap, that'll send their stock soaring," he bragged to Robert Richards.

Even though he was still ambivalent about getting back into the business, Drew's filmmaking instincts continued to function. He couldn't just make a three-minute short. It simply had no flow to it. "What I did was shoot the scene as a regular scene for a feature. I took only three minutes of the hottest stuff, and I had the rest of it that I could use at some point in the future, if I ever wanted to."

The truth was that, in his heart of hearts, Drew desperately wanted to get back into filmmaking. It had been his life for years, and nothing else inspired him. "I truly love working with film and video," he told Jerry Douglas. "That's the bottom line. You can make all the money in the world, and if you're not doing what you want to do, it's not fulfilling. So I said, 'There must be a way of eroticizing safe sex and getting across a message and keeping people alive.' And that's how *Turbo Charge* came about."

The truth of the matter is that *Turbo Charge* is something of a schizophrenic hybrid. At the beginning there is the claim "Safe sex can be fun—and hot," but then the film goes on to show many acts that aren't necessarily representative of safer sex. The safe segment is the complete scene with Al and Justin Cade that Drew had excerpted for his Swiss-government effort. Additional scenes include a self-suck solo and a segment that pairs Al with James Williams, the black man whose pump-distended penis Drew would feature in two additional films.

"James was a customer who ordered a cylinder from the pump company that was so large, I couldn't believe it. Keith gave me his name, and by cross-checking with my own files, I found out he was also a Surge client. I called him up and asked him if he would be interested in doing a video." Critics of the film found the kink quite convincing but criticized it for only giving lip service to the concept of safer sex. Still, it was a beginning.

Drew's new relationship was already beginning to show signs of strain. Looking at photos of Cade, one cannot help but be struck by his physical resemblance to Richard. Coloring, body type, even his facial features, are hauntingly familiar. If Drew thought he had found a sort of reincarnation of Richard, the resemblance was only superficial.

"Living together strained our relationship," Cade told me. "Drew had told me about his HIV status the night we met, so we were limited regarding what we could do sexually. This was doubly true, because as a Canadian, I had to stay negative or run the risk of being deported. I was also bothered by the celebrity bit at times. To tell the truth, I felt jealousy when Drew would be with other people. We did three-ways and larger groups. I wasn't crazy about it, but Drew craved it, so I went along. He was sexually driven and fooled around a lot with a lot of different guys, which really didn't bother me unless he was with someone I knew. Then it was harder to deal with."

Keith Reiter remembered Cade's attitude vividly. "When Drew first introduced me to Justin, he wanted us to have a three-way. We went to bed together, and Justin kept physically pushing me away. He was extremely jealous. I never got over that."

By May 1988, after a year and a half together, Justin and Drew decided to call it quits. "Drew moved to San Francisco to be with Keith. He needed a change. He went up north, and I went to Venice Beach and became a real beach person. I always stayed in contact with Drew. In fact, our relationship got better after we were no longer living together."

As proof of this amicability, Justin appeared in Drew's next Surge production, *A Night Alone With Al Parker*. "Any time Drew did a movie when I was around, I'd agree to fill in if he was short a performer or if I was short on cash. I never really wanted to be a porn star, but I liked to help Drew out."

This feature was a compilation effort. As Drew explained during an interview, "What happened was, I had all this footage I'd shot years before but hadn't used for one reason or another. It had remained unused because I didn't like the way my hair looked or really silly things like that. So I said to myself, 'Well, in this day and age when you can't do anything anymore, why not? If it's because I don't like the way my hair looks, I can get over that.' "

The premise of the film is that when a date cancels, Al Parker reminisces about his past sexual encounters. These include a hot scene in a barn with J. D. Slater; a three-way with Justin Cade and Daniel Holt in which Al looks uncharacteristically paunchy and out of shape (no wonder he hadn't used this footage); and footage of Al sucking off a host of anonymous uncut cocks in a tearoom setting. A highlight of the film is the footage that binds the various loops together—Al fucking himself with his cock, his balls, and a dildo. "Scott Taylor had taught me that trick in *Turned On*. I fucked myself with my dick and balls, which is what I ran home and did immediately after we shot that movie. I had never even thought of doing that before, and I thought it was a fairly neat trick. No one had ever seen me do that before, and it certainly is safe.

"For somebody who isn't a bottom, it was surprisingly easy. I guess if it's you doing it, it's completely different. The only thing that's interesting about being able to stick your balls up your ass is that when you come, your prostate spasms, which makes your sphincter close, which drags your balls up your butt and presses them against the prostate—so it's very much like a continuous circle. The only problem is after you've come, you've got these big balls up your butt, and it's not easy to get them out."

In an interview Drew gave Robert Richards in September 1988—the third of his interviews with Richards—his view of *A Night Alone With Al Parker* was considerably darker. "I guess the films I'm doing now are basically about tying up loose ends. *Night Alone* is a compilation of older things. When I looked at them, I realized they could be put together as a nice safe-sex film—that by adding an on-camera narration I could make a nice, healthy movie out of the various pieces. However, when I showed the final product to distributors, they wanted nothing to do with it. They wouldn't even consider it. They told me I was hitting the viewer over the head with a message he didn't want to hear.

"So there I was, with the first film I'd done in a long time, and no distributor would even touch it. So I had to recut it and add to it, and now I make no pretense at all that it's trying to be a safe-sex film. I know I'm going to get a lot of flak, because for a long while I've been expounding that the sex practices shown on film must be safe, and now I come out with a movie that seems to endorse unsafe sex. I hope people don't start throwing rocks when they see me."

CHAPTER SEVENTEEN

San Francisco

In 1988 Drew sold the house in Hermosa Beach that had served as both home and studio for him and Richard, then moved north to San Francisco. Keith Reiter was there, waiting to welcome him. He moved in with Keith and remained as friend and lover for the rest of his life. "We really loved each other," Keith told me. "We cared for each other, even bought a home together. In San Francisco we have domestic partnerships, and Drew suggested we register as such. We never got around to that, but we did have a loving, long-term sexual relationship."

Keith's penis-pump business was booming, and with Drew there to work with him in production and sales, the money came pouring in. The pair bought a place in San Francisco and began refurbishing it. "It was a fabulous palace of a place, all marble and gold and skylights," Drew's father declared, waxing ecstatic. "It's actually a small two-bedroom row house," Keith informed me. Nevertheless, it was a very comfortable home that gave the pair a perfect venue for entertaining.

"They were very adept at entertaining," Ted Sawicki told me. "They threw wonderful dinners and parties for their friends." Jerry Douglas remembered going to one of their dinner parties in the late '80s. "Once I went there and Drew was in an apron, bustling around the house à la Martha Stewart, fixing dinner. It was so funny to see butch Al Parker as a hostess."

Keith was able to fulfill many of the functions that Richard had taken care of for so many years, shielding Drew from some of life's harsher realities. "Drew was a terrible businessman," Keith said. "He was great with the spending, however, and a lot of people tried to take advantage of that. In 1988, when Drew started making movies here in San Francisco, he met a fellow named Rick Lewis who worked for a big gay-film distributing group. Rick was interested in movies and got Drew back into making films."

Drew thought Rick was a great guy and credited him with getting Surge Studio up and running again. "He really convinced me that there was a need for me to keep Surge going," Drew told Robert Richards during the course of their final interview. "And if it hadn't been for him, I probably wouldn't be doing it."

Unfortunately, in addition to helping Drew, Rick was also helping himself. "The guy was ripping checks out of the back of the Surge Studio checkbook to buy his drugs. He also used Drew and Surge for his own sexual purposes. He'd tell guys, 'Have sex with me, and I'll take you to Al Parker's house.' He brought a whole parade of people through the house till I got wind of it and put a stop to it. Richard had taken care of that aspect of life in the early days. I did it in the later part of Drew's life. He needed to be protected from himself. I don't mean that in a negative sense.

It was just that he was a little too open, too trusting of people."

Which was not to imply that Drew was a flake. He was dedicated to his craft and worked hard. "It didn't matter to him if you called at 3 in the morning to order a film. If you ordered it today, it would go out the next morning. When Drew was working, he was organized and totally dedicated."

When he was working, it was often in the guise of Al Parker, the most successful product that the enterprising young man from Natick ever created. "I never really knew Al Parker," Reiter told me, "although he did exist. Whenever Drew would try to get grand on me—which only happened when he was being Al—I'd remind him that there wasn't really an Al Parker. I know now that I was wrong. Drew created Al Parker. In public he would become Al for his fans. When we went out people would come up to the table at dinner, pull up a chair, and want to talk. He always understood the importance of these people in terms of his career. Generally, they weren't so much hitting on him as idolizing him. I found it quite tiresome, but Drew was unfailingly gracious."

In spite of the fact that he had met literally thousands of people over the years, Drew lived a quiet life in San Francisco. "Drew knew movie stars, producers, directors—the whole spectrum of the Hollywood film business, but he seldom got in touch with them, and they certainly didn't come around to visit him." Reiter mused. "I think they were afraid to be identified with a man who was so recognizably a porn star."

One concrete example of this phobia occurred when Drew tried to get a part in the film *Pacific Heights,* which director John Schlesinger had under development. Drew approached him time and again, but Schlesinger, whom Drew had known for years through the director's photographer lover, wouldn't give him the time of day.

Drew's personal habits were quite regular for such an icon of life in the gay fast lane. "Drew didn't drink at all," Reiter said, "not even wine with dinner. He was a good old-fashioned pothead. Drew smoked dope continually. Every 15 minutes he'd take a hit of dope. I still have his pipe." Drew was crazy about his pipe. "He and Richard were in Canada once and left the pipe in a hotel room. They hit the road and went over 100 miles when Drew discovered it was missing. He made Richard turn around and go back because of all the beautiful men who had had their lips on it."

Drew went looking for most of his sex during the day. He was an early riser, and most evenings he was in bed by 9 o'clock. Both Reiter and Justin Cade attest to Drew's habit of snuggling into bed early and watching TV. The animated sitcom *The Simpsons* was new then, and it was one of his favorites to watch at bedtime.

After Drew had settled in with Keith in San Francisco and hooked up with Rick Lewis, he was soon back at work creating yet another Surge classic. *Better Than Ever,* his first movie shot directly on video, was well-received by critics and the public. It was strange for Drew because it was the first full-scale production he had done without Richard. "He was the business end of our business, and I was the creative end. All of a sudden, I had to do everything. And it just isn't as much fun for me if I don't have somebody to share it with. The whole thing that was fun about building Surge Studio was building it with somebody that I loved and watching this thing grow into a viable business. Fortunately, I was working with people I'd been working with for years, and I think everybody was so happy about putting death behind them and doing a production that everything just clicked. It was like a family getting together again."

Better Than Ever was built around Joe Cade, whose face and physique bear an uncanny resemblance to Michelangelo's David. Cade, who had won the gold medal for best physique in the heavyweight class at the '86 Gay Games, has fond memories of working with Drew. "I met him through Justin Cade, who had been my lover several years previously. Justin and Drew were dating at the time.

"I always thought Drew was an incredibly sweet, down-to-earth, supportive guy. He was always there for people. He was also a driven businessman and had his priorities and goals well-organized. He was very involved with selling the penis pumps. When we were all in New York for the *Donahue* show, Drew walked in and out of the stores taking orders. He'd only be gone for what seemed a few seconds, then he'd come out with a two- or three-thousand-dollar order under his belt. Big business in a very short period of time.

"Drew wasn't impressed by his fame. One of the things I admired most about him was that he was oblivious to people staring at him. He knew how he affected people, but he wasn't impressed by himself. The fame is fleeting, and he knew that.

"Since Drew was an actor himself, he was patient on the set. He gave you time to do the work. The downside of that was that he could sometimes let things go on too long before demanding that people get back on track. He was very relaxing to work with. He'd tell us what he wanted up front, and if it wasn't working out he'd tell us, but he wouldn't be nasty about it. He never rode your butt about things."

James Williams, the black guy with the cock so grotesquely distended by the penis pump, is featured in the first scene, costarring with an average-looking blond guy with a big dick. The scene plays out as a how-to guide for safe sex.

Joe Cade is featured in a three-way scenario with Brian

Adams and David DaBello, which soon develops into a duo between Cade and Adams. The chemistry between these two is palpable—Drew was quite pleased about it. "They met on our set and hit it off. They're still together."

The next scene features Drew, who makes it quite clear that he wants his nuts tortured. He's not kidding. As anyone who has seen his films can attest, Al Parker had a cock and balls that could be pulled any way but off. The sex is safe, using condoms even for cock sucking. At one point his partner swallows Parker's imposing cock and balls simultaneously. Al fingers the guy, then fucks him on the hood of his car with his balls and his cock.

The film concludes with an orgy sequence that seems truncated. The filming technique is good, employing facial shots and clear, focused close-ups of the sexual action, but abrupt edits spoil the flow of the scene. Suddenly, Drew runs on-screen and calls out, "It's a wrap." The actors applaud, and the film ends.

When asked by Jerry Douglas whether he required his performers to use rubbers, Drew was adamant. "They don't like them. Nobody likes them. But, quite frankly, if you don't want to use a rubber, I don't want you in the movie."

Drew's claim is somewhat dubious. Condoms are used, but if you blink, you'll miss them. Despite Drew's claims to the contrary, this film doesn't make any great strides toward eroticizing safe sex. Drew uses condoms in his scenes, even for oral sex, but the other performers do not. When there is anal penetration, the condom covers only the head of the cock, leaving the whole operation in a rather precarious state.

Shortly after wrapping up production on *Better Than Ever* Drew got a call from Justin. Justin had been invited to appear on *Donahue* and wondered if Drew would be interested in appearing as well. The whole show that day in October 1988 was spent interviewing six men who made gay-porn films— Tim Ross, Tim Cramer, Brian Adams, Joe Cade, Justin Cade, and last, but far from least, Al Parker.

Drew acquitted himself quite well, using the show as a forum for his views on safe sex and the state of the porn industry. He fielded questions from Donahue and the audience alike, making a stand for the legitimacy of his career. "What started out to be a fluffy, frivolous form of entertainment has become a serious educational tool for us. We are doing for our people what the government would not do. We are showing in graphic ways what you can and cannot do sexually to protect yourself against infection. I am doing this to educate people on how to behave now—on how to avoid infection with the AIDS virus."

Drew defended his work vigorously, making it clear that his was a business like any other: driven by market demand. "If people weren't interested, there'd be no product to sell." He also asserted that safe sex, like anything else, must be taught, not just talked about. "We need to educate young people and show what they can and can't do sexually. You can tell somebody to use a condom, but if you don't show them how to use it, it is like giving out the keys to the car without any driving lessons."

When asked if he had managed to avoid infection, Drew hedged and stated that he was perfectly healthy. It was a stance he maintained to the bitter end. As Keith recalled, Drew viewed it as a matter of necessity. "We were in Puerto Rico one time, and Drew left his AZT in the room when we checked out of a hotel. When we went back, he indicated that the drugs were mine. He definitely didn't want anyone to find out that he had AIDS, because it would have ruined his career."

Drew went on to fight the standard battles gays face when confronting the straight world—Christian fundamentalists touting abstinence as the cure for all ills; a man questioning why animals weren't gay if it was a normal state of grace; a woman asking if he became gay because he had been traumatized as a child—and acquitted himself with grace and skill. He probably converted no one in the audience to the side of gay porn, but he was an excellent spokesperson for the cause.

During the show Drew made public the split with his sister that had occurred after she learned that Richard had AIDS—and found support for his position from the audience. He also told the story of how his father had discovered he was an actor in pornographic films. "He went into a bookstore and saw my face on the cover of a magazine. He called me up and asked if it was really me. I asked him what he was doing looking at gay magazines in a bookstore. He just asked if I was happy and if I was making money." What Drew didn't tell Donahue, but did tell Robert Richards, was that his dad also said, "I'm glad to see you inherited my dick."

As is often the case with gay men, Drew's relationship with his father was sometimes troubled. As a youngster his father's job kept him on the road and away from home. Later, when Drew had accepted his homosexuality, he kept his father at arm's length, especially after he began his career in porn. After he moved to California, his father came to visit, and Drew told him he was gay. "I accepted it," Mr. Okun told me. "It didn't change my relationship with him."

Years later, after his dad had stumbled across that fateful magazine, their relationship became much more open. Robert Richards said Drew told him he "was quite distressed when his father told him that he knew what he was doing for a living, because he had always tried to keep that part of his life separate. I think he was relieved that his father reacted as well as he did."

After Drew moved to San Francisco, his dad became a regular visitor. "I visited him four times a year for the last five years of his life. I was really close to him." On one of those visits, his dad discovered the pumps. "My father, who is 70 years old, came to visit. We have a shop here in the house because the pumps are all handmade, and he found out what they were and took one home with him. He became an aficionado, and he's actually gotten us accounts in New York. He'll go into a dirty bookstore and he'll say, 'Do you have this Original San Francisco Pump?' And if the guy says no, he'll pull out the brochures and try to make a sale."

Keith recalls a quite different version of the relationship between Drew and his father. "He and his father never got along when Drew was younger. Even after they reconciled, Drew dreaded when he would come here. I tried to make peace and invited him frequently. The thought of an approaching visit would tie Drew's stomach up in knots.

"When Drew first discovered he was HIV-positive he told his dad and asked him not to tell anybody. Well, his father went to Boston and started blabbing it around to people. Drew found out and swore he'd never say another word to him about it. He never did, although I secretly kept his father abreast of what was happening with him."

Then there was the little matter of the business. When Mr. Okun came to visit, he would work along with Keith and Drew, helping to assemble and distribute the pumps. "After Drew died his dad tried to steal my business. He now manufactures pumps under the logo of Boston Pump Works." According to Justin Cade, Mr. Okun even tried to lure some of

Keith's clients away from him. Mr. Okun didn't care to discuss
the subject, noting only that "Keith and I aren't friendly. I
haven't contacted him for over five years. In the end, he took
over Drew's life."

Just a few months after wrapping up *Better Than Ever,* Drew
was behind—and in front of—the camera again, this time to
make *Surge Men Are Very Receptive.* All the Surge trademarks
are clearly in evidence—plenty of foreskin, autofellatio, Al
doing the old fuck 'em–with-cock-and-balls routine, and the
now-ubiquitous pump. The movie looks good, and so does Al,
who appears in the first and last scenes. Al is wearing his matu-
rity well. He's still got the body and can make all the right sexual moves. The final scene, in which Al turns Butch Taylor
every way but loose, is a paradigm of hot, raunchy sex. The
camera work and lighting are very good throughout, catching
all the details without becoming overly clinical.

Drew had enlisted Justin Cade, who turns in a memorable
performance as a dispatcher for a cable TV company. He
appears on-screen and immediately pulls out a display case
containing sample products of the San Francisco Pump
Works. He gets a pump set up and ready to use. It quickly
transpires that he is doing an extended ad for the pump in a
solo session that is used to bind all the other scenes together.
Every time Justin reappears, his cock gets bigger. He also
pumps up his nipples and his foreskin to enormous proportions. By the time he finally climaxes, his cock is flopping
around like a third leg. Based on the evidence in this film, the
pump is indeed effective.

With this film, Drew realized that the business was changing radically. Even the Al Parker imprimatur was no longer a
guarantee of profitability. "The video business has changed to

the point now where a good film doesn't necessarily make money because of the pirated duplicates and the glut of product on the market." It was becoming increasingly difficult for a small independent company to turn out two or three films a year and survive.

Drew already had another movie on the drawing board, employing a format that cut production costs to virtually nothing. *Surge Men at Their Very Best* was a compilation film, combining snippets from *Better Than Ever, Turbo Charge, A Night Alone With Al Parker,* and *Surge Men Are Very Receptive.* The only justification for the film was the final scene, which featured the first public outing of Drew's restored foreskin. Always fascinated by that little sleeve of skin, he had long wanted one of his own and had finally found someone to give it to him.

"I had what's called a reconstruction," he told Jerry Douglas. "It wasn't grafted from anywhere. When I was circumcised, they did what was called a dorsal-slit circumcision, so what they did was pull over what was left of it and reattach it. A straight Jewish doctor did it for me, and as odd as it sounds, he'd never done it before." (That could only have sounded odd to Drew.) "He doesn't know who I am or what I do. I didn't tell him. He did a beautiful job, and you would never be able to tell."

Although he was ecstatic about the new foreskin, he did admit that it was a lot of work to keep clean. Beyond the maintenance, he was delighted by the effect when he was having sex. "There's a lot more to play with," he burbled enthusiastically. He also admitted that the actual operation had been a painful three-step process that had put him out of commission for months. "I couldn't even get a hard-on for three weeks. I thought a lot about baseball scores. I was very apprehensive. I didn't know if it was going to work. I mean, for Al Parker to fuck around with his dick is a very risky thing. That is the way I make my living, after all."

Keith remembered the whole ordeal vividly. "The day he had the operation was sheer hell for me. He was literally walking around the house banging his head on the wall, moaning about how he had ruined himself for life. He was so bad that I threatened to move to a hotel for the night."

In the final analysis, however, Drew announced to the world that it had all been worthwhile. "It's like having a new dick after 36 years. If I can't go out and have a good time with everybody, I'm going to have my dick the way I like it, and then I won't mind playing with myself. Not that I minded playing with myself before, but truthfully, it's like playing with somebody else, you know?"

Throughout his life Drew never lacked for sexual playmates. "His sex life was never-ending," Keith confided with a wry chuckle. "He could cruise 24 hours a day. He even had ads in swinger magazines under different names. Drew had an absolutely enormous sex drive."

This drive was constantly getting him into trouble. The run-in with the authorities at Disney wasn't Drew's only brush with the men entrusted with keeping tearooms pure. "We were in New York, and Drew was cruising in the Madison Square Garden train station. He was hanging out in one of the bathrooms, and the cops came in and busted him. He had a bag of weed in his pocket when they took him to the cop station in the building. Fortunately for him, they let him go and didn't find the weed."

Then there was the time at Venice Beach when Drew was busted in a tearoom by the seashore on Halloween. "It was right after he had his foreskin restoration. When he went to court, he told the judge about his operation and claimed that he was only showing the other guy in the tearoom how it worked. After several court appearances, he managed to charm his way out of it."

Charm failed him, however, during an encounter with a very famous dancer. Rudolf Nureyev was in Los Angeles, and the man in charge of the famous artist's stay decided for some unknown reason that Drew—or Al Parker, to be more precise—should be his tour guide. Drew was interested because he had heard that Nureyev had a big dick. Needless to say, he was all excited about meeting him—and getting him in the sack. "They met, and it was a disaster," Reiter recalled. "All Drew wanted to talk about was sex, and all Nureyev wanted to talk about was dance. My take on it was that they both viewed themselves as the prima donna, and neither man was willing to play second fiddle. Finally, Nureyev blew up. He lobbed a can of Coke at Drew and threw him out of his hotel suite. Then he went out and toured L.A. by himself."

When the '90s started Drew was busy on both sides of the camera, increasingly as producer for other filmmakers and as a guest performer for other studios. The last films in which Drew wore all three hats—actor, producer, director—were *Kinky Stuff* and *America's Sexiest Home Videos,* and even these were compilations of Drew's existing footage mixed with loops supplied by exhibitionistic amateurs.

In *America's Sexiest Home Videos* men from across the country check in with scenes of masturbation, cock sucking and fucking. The film primarily features vacuum-pumped pricks, giving the overall impression of an X-rated infomercial for the San Francisco Pump Works. Al Parker appears in the last scene for foreskin play and fucking with Grant Lance.

Kinky Stuff, a catalog of sexual freaks and specialists in the bizarre, is primarily memorable for the first scene. The star of this segment, a not particularly well-built or attractive blond, is an autofellatio maniac. After rubbing his cock over his belly, chest, and nipples, he almost literally folds himself in half and swallows his own penis right down to the balls. He ends this show-stopping performance by erupting like a geyser, literally covering a full-length mirror with his load.

The scenes that follow are all obviously home-video quality, displaying various styles of kink: balls tied till they turn purple, pumped cocks that flop like third legs, and a cock with a 90-degree downturn. In the final scene Al Parker costars for the third time with James Williams and his grotesquely distended genitals. Bearded and youthful, Al still looks good. He doesn't use a condom for sucking, but dons one later when he fucks Williams.

As Drew's involvement with film tapered off he took an increasingly activist stance, often using his celebrity status as a gay icon to promote safer sex and to raise money for AIDS-related causes. When asked to help out at gay fund-raisers, Drew always made every effort to comply. He attended the 1987 March on Washington and addressed the crowd at a rally. In 1990 he was grand marshal in the Boston Gay Pride parade.

He also had a large European following and was treated like a real star by his fans there. "Drew and I went to Europe to open a bookstore," Keith recalled. "It was all arranged through a company in L.A. They offered to pay Drew's way to Amsterdam, and he negotiated for me to go along as well. We did the circuit of gay European capitals, including Berlin, where Drew was received as a big star. It was great for his ego to have so many men swarming around him."

As the pair returned to the United States, Drew ran afoul of customs in Seattle. "A customs agent got very nasty with Drew. She found his AZT in his luggage and began questioning him. The exchange became heated, and before it was over, she threatened to cut up his favorite coat to check for illicit drugs. Afterward, he vowed never to leave the country again."

Drew's health was beginning to decline, but the ravages of the disease remained hidden. He fought back, scrupulously keeping up his regimen of exercise and maintaining his Southern California tan even in the frequently overcast Bay Area. That he succeeded so well is a testament to good genes and sheer determination. Right up to his last film appearances he remained the quintessential macho man, the stud, the perfect clone.

"I never knew he was sick," recalled Blue Blake, an actor, writer, and director. "He looked great when I met him. So it was a great shock when he did die. I dated Drew. I had been named Mr. Drummer of the U.K., and I came to San Francisco to compete in the world finals in 1990. Drew—or, rather, Al Parker—was one of the judges. I was out and about, having a great time in the city. Well, when I got back to my hotel, there was a message that said Al Parker wanted to meet me. I called the number, he showed up about ten minutes later, and we jumped right into bed together.

"I remember thinking the first time I went to bed with him, 'God, I can't believe I'm in bed with this man.' I told my friends in London, and they were very impressed. When he phoned me up the next day and we went out together, I felt very special being around him.

"I think Drew was happy in San Francisco. All the guys

there were emulating him. He had created the clone look. He was so successful at it, as a matter of fact, that if you had seen him walking down the street and he hadn't been Al Parker, you wouldn't have looked twice. He looked pretty much like all the other clones in the city at the time. No matter where you went, people would stop and want to talk to him, to tell him how good his movies were. I got the feeling they were all dying to get him into bed. Many of them managed it.

"He wasn't actually my type. I'd been dating a lot of pro bodybuilders, and Drew was tiny by contrast. I don't think I was his type either. He liked older guys with mustaches. But he also liked muscle guys, and I was pumped. I was also uncut. Drew was obsessed with foreskin, especially his own foreskin reattachment. That was definitely part of the attraction between us.

"We'd go to the gym together to work out, and I remember I'd get pissed at him. He had a great upper body, but he wouldn't train his legs, and as a result they were pretty spindly. He told me he thought skinny legs made his dick look bigger. It was really silly.

"He was short, only about 5 foot 8, and so his dick looked even bigger than it was. I remember he'd always wear a cock ring to the gym, and out on the street he'd wear these tight jeans, and his dick would be hanging to his knee. I had the impression that it would've been really nice if he could have gotten beyond the fact that he had a big dick. It became the central reality of his life.

"Drew had basically retired from the business when I met him, and [had] gone on to promoting his cock pumps. He was a really successful businessman. He also had these terrific ideas for films. He was very creative. He'd been around when people were doing porn for the fun of it, not just for the money. Porn was less of a business when he started out, and most of the guys in the films really were gay. It wasn't like it is today.

"It was important for Drew to be Al Parker. He got off on the fame and the recognition. I've met a lot of porn stars who are like that. Unfortunately, these guys begin to believe their publicity. In the end, we drifted apart—we were from different worlds. I was still in the Marines, and I had to go back to England and join my platoon. That's how we lost contact. When I heard about him again, he had died."

Keeping Al Parker going was part of what kept Drew going in his last years. After every bout with illness Drew would fight his way back, striving to keep the legend intact. Keith watched him struggle. "For the last two years of his life Drew never complained, even though there were real horrors on his horizon. He had headaches and was exhausted much of the time, but he soldiered on. His ophthalmologist had found cytomegalovirus, and there was Kaposi's sarcoma developing in his throat. When he had gone to be grand marshal of the gay parade in Boston he got deathly ill, and I had to fly out and get him and bring him home."

Even with all of this going on, Drew-as-Al created a stir wherever he went. One afternoon, when he was at the ophthalmologist's office for a cytomegalovirus treatment, his presence caused such a buzz in the waiting room that even the doctor was aware of it. He came out and saw that Drew was the center of attention. "Who is that?" he asked a patient. "You don't know?" the astounded man replied. "Why, that's the Liz Taylor of the gay-film world."

If the recognition was bracing for Drew, the opposite

response shook him to his core. A few months before his death, he and Keith were out walking in San Francisco's Castro district. "There were a couple of guys behind us," Keith said. "One leaned over to his buddy and said, 'Look! There's Al Parker.' His pal retorted, 'Who the hell is that?' Drew heard and was devastated."

Drew was ready to show the world just who the hell Al Parker was one final time. He was asked by Falcon to appear in the film *Overload,* which was released in 1992, shortly before his death. The final scene with Al and Craig Slater opens with a plug for his pump business. Craig Slater calls him up and asks if a porn legend like Al ever gets together with people. Al's reply isn't hard to guess.

The upper body is still very defined, the face is relatively unlined, and the famous cock looks meaner than ever, yet Drew definitely looks older. As the scene progresses he goes through the motions, but much of the fire is gone. His skin is pale and waxy-looking, and he no longer has the luminescent quality that was so much a part of his mystique. Still, he carries on, pumping his cock and balls to near-grotesque proportions. He fucks Slater, then fists him and shoots his load on Slater's sweat-slick torso. It was Drew's last appearance before the cameras.

There was one other film project that Drew had been urged to consider during his last years. Award-winning director Jerry Douglas had crafted a script with Drew in mind. "I originally wrote my film *Family Values* for Drew. He came to me and told me he couldn't do the film because he had only recently discovered that he was HIV-positive. As a result, Douglas shelved the film until 1998, when it was released to great critical acclaim, starring Derrick Stanton in the role originally envisioned for Drew. It was a role with real substance that would almost certainly have enhanced the Parker legend.

CHAPTER EIGHTEEN

Last Days

On June 25, 1992, Drew celebrated his 40th birthday with a small group of friends at his home in San Francisco. There was a cake, and Keith read some doggerel verses written by Drew's father. Drew blew out his candles, then pushed away the cake in mock horror. "I don't want to be 40!" he shrieked in an outraged falsetto. "But ya are," a friend shrieked back, à la Bette Davis. On the videotape Drew is still handsome, although somewhat thin, and appears in good spirits.

August 6 was Justin Cade's birthday, and he had asked Drew to join him in Los Angeles. Drew drove down for the occasion, although he wasn't feeling well. He dropped in to see Cousin Janie, and she noticed that he looked really ill, but he didn't complain, so she just tried to enjoy their time together.

Cade also noticed that Drew was deteriorating. "We ate with friends the night of my birthday at Marina Del Rey, and I remember thinking how drawn he looked. We went back to my place, and Drew sat on the edge of the bed. His eyes looked different. There was no sparkle in them. He was looking in the mirror, and he said, 'I may not even be here next week.' I dropped to my knees and put my head on his knees and cried. He looked so different, like his spirit was already gone. He said to me, 'You act like you'll never see me again.' I put my arms around him and held him.

"The next day he left and drove back to San Francisco. I asked him not to go. It was really hot, and the air conditioning in his van was broken. He looked so weak and drawn. He got home on Tuesday, and when I called him he seemed a little better. I'd never gone for more than two or three days without talking to him, but for some reason I didn't call over the weekend, which was really odd. Then Keith called me at work and told me Drew had died."

Keith saw the end approaching but was powerless to stop it. "Drew went to the gym right up to the end of his life. He died on a Monday morning, and he had been to the gym that previous Saturday. He woke up that morning and had a flat tire. He tried to change it but was too weak, so I changed it for him. Then he drove to the gym but didn't have the strength do his workout. He came home and went to bed. We had dinner guests that night, and Drew dragged himself out of bed and played the host. He was in bed all day Sunday, too weak to get up.

"On Monday morning he woke up freezing. He couldn't get warm, so he wanted to take a hot bath before his doctor's appointment. He started filling the Jacuzzi, and I went downstairs to my office. The water kept running for such a long time that I went to check on him. He had slipped down into the tub and was so weak, he couldn't pull himself up to turn off the water. He tried to call out but couldn't shout loud enough to make me hear him. When I got to him the water was less than an inch from his nose. I dried him off and put him back to bed.

"I had to carry him out to the van later so I could drive him to the doctor's office. On the way he told me to take him to the hospital. I rushed him to the emergency room, and ten minutes later he was dead. I had power of health [a medical power of attorney] and made the decision not to use heroic measures on him. It was the hardest thing I ever did in my life, but Drew was ready to go."

For the last several months of his life Drew had been very worried about how he looked. "We were out one day driving around, and he turned to me and said, 'Keith, I want to ask a question, and I want you to be honest with me. Do I look like I have AIDS?' Just the day before we had been at San Gregorio Beach. Drew had gotten into pumping his dick and wearing spandex to show off the massive bulge. I remembered watching him walk down the beach and thinking his ass and legs were totally emaciated. It made me sad because it accentuated the signs of his illness. I so much wanted to answer no to his question, but I couldn't."

Drew had often said he wanted to die young. "I'd rather be remembered as being young, vibrant, good-looking, and active than to be an 88-year-old person and just a leftover." He got his wish. Andrew Robert Okun exited this life on August 17, 1992.

A memorial service was held for Drew at the home he and Keith had shared in San Francisco. "It was amazing," Keith said. "People came from all over to attend—Los Angeles, Salt Lake City, Key West. And these weren't Drew's close friends— you'd expect his friends to come—but these were fans of his who had traveled across country to pay their respects. There were two men turned out in Royal Canadian Mounted Police regalia—one a friend, one a fan who had never met him—who formed an honor guard over Drew's ashes. So Drew spent his memorial service perched in a picture window overlooking San Francisco, surrounded by handsome men in uniform. He would have loved the drama of it all."

A few weeks later Keith and a few friends drove out to San Gregorio Beach to scatter Drew's ashes. That was where he wanted to be, he had told Keith. "I took the lid off the urn and tossed his ashes into the air. The wind caught them, and they blew right back in my fucking face." Drew, as usual, had the final laugh.

Drew was remembered fondly by his friends and colleagues. For Cousin Janie, he was "good-hearted, down-to-earth, honest. He genuinely cared about other people. Drew was very bright and creative, with an interesting take on life."

His father remembered his son as a "generous man and a successful and innovative filmmaker."

"I can't tell you an unpleasant thing about him," Robert Richards said. "He lived his life on an amazingly steady course, considering the business and the icon he became in that business. He was level-headed and very smart."

"Drew was funny beyond belief," Keith Reiter remembered. "He would start to mimic the news, and he would have me rolling on the floor. We loved each other very much."

Business associate Dave Brunner admired Drew for his business acumen. "As a producer, I'd say he stands out more than any other because he produced, directed, and acted in his own films."

To Ted Sawicki, "Drew was such a hot guy. He was really comfortable to be around. He was always easy to work with and had a wicked sense of humor."

Gino Colbert, one of Drew's colleagues in the X-rated film

industry, was "quite a fan of his. He was a pioneer in this business, because he crossed over from acting to having his own company. He was a trendsetter."

Justin Cade summed it up quite poignantly: "I've never stopped loving him or caring for him. I'd give anything to have him back."

That, of course, isn't possible. However, Drew Okun—or at least his alter ego, Al Parker—is still very much with us. In an industry whose product measures its shelf life in weeks rather than years, Al Parker and titles from his Surge Productions are still available—and still frequently viewed. His picture still arrests the eye. His performances still arouse. For as long as libidos rage out of control, Al Parker will be there to scratch the itch, his luminous presence flickering on-screen as he effortlessly turns on yet another generation of horny viewers.

VIDEOGRAPHY

The Early Loops

Challenger, Brentwood
Chute, Colt
Timberwolves I & II, Colt
Hand Tooled, Colt
Scout's Honor, Starline
Weekend Lockup, FalconPac #4
Rocks and Hard Places, FalconPac #19
Taxi, Falcon Pac #3

The Early Features

Heavy Equipment, Advocate Video
The Other Side of Aspen, FalconPac #1
Inches, Steve Scott
Wanted, Steve Scott
Performance (Cameo), Steve Scott

The Surge Films

Flashback, 1981

Turned On, 1982
Games, 1983
Dangerous, 1983
A Few Good Men, 1983
One in a Billion, 1984
Rangers, 1984
Head Trips, 1985
Strange Places, Strange Things, 1985
Hard Disk Drive, 1985
Therapy, 1985
Oversize Load, 1986
Century Mining, 1986
High Tech, 1986
Turbo Charge, 1988
A Night Alone With Al Parker, 1988
Surge Men Are Better Than Ever, 1989
Surge Men Are Very Receptive, 1989
Surge Men at Their Very Best, 1990
America's Sexiest Home Videos, 1990
Kinky Stuff, 1990
Overload, FalconPac #77

Interview Videos—Nonsexual

Gay Voices, Gay Legends
Advocate Men Live 2

Drew sold the rights to most of the Surge features after Richard's death, and enterprising marketing types have been splicing scenes together ever since. This accounts for a number of compilation films on the shelves that were not edited by Drew and which are not listed. All of the Colt and Falcon titles are still readily available. The Surge titles are available through Bijou Video. I was, unfortunately, not able to locate a copy of *Scout's Honor* for viewing while I researched this book.